# PRAISE FOR HANNIBAL B. JOHNSON

"Social justice is recognizing that even if you think you're the chosen one, you're never the only one. Until you come to my side of the fence to see what I see and I come to your side to see what you see, we will struggle with social justice. Johnson's book will help get us there."

— **JC WATTS**, *POLITICIAN, CLERGYMAN, BUSINESSMAN, AND ATHLETE*

"Hannibal B. Johnson is a powerful and authentic voice for truth and constructive action for racial equity. His approach of honest introspection, community engagement, and collaborative advocacy offers an effective framework. This is a practical handbook for those seeking to heal and rebuild their communities."

— **ROB CORCORAN**, *TRAINING CONSULTANT, INITIATIVES OF CHANGE INTERNATIONAL; FOUNDER EMERITUS, HOPE IN THE CITIES; AND AUTHOR*

"As a social justice lion, Johnson provides a thought-provoking, clear vision for advancing social justice. This is a must-read for anyone wanting to learn more about how they can make a difference in their lives and communities."

— **LURA HAMMOND**, *EXECUTIVE DIRECTOR, ASSOCIATION OF LEADERSHIP PROFESSIONALS*

"The work of attaining social justice is without end. It is a complicated and ongoing process that requires persistent attention. We, as human beings, are all made better by contributing to its advancement. The results can be stronger families, communities, and nations. Hannibal B. Johnson gives us the tools needed to stay on track and take practical steps towards social justice and the consequent uplifting of society and humanity."

— **BILL ANOATUBBY,** *GOVERNOR, CHICKASAW NATION*

"In the heart of Oklahoma, my friend Hannibal Johnson is giving us a template to better navigate our complex world. It is a chance to better understand social justice and what it means for communities, like Native Americans, that have faced historical traumas and have been marginalized over time. This is an important book highlighting the need for inclusion, awareness, and active participation so that we can all live in a more fair and equal society. One of our core Cherokee cultural values teaches us to is to value and be responsible for one another. That is an idea Hannibal has also tapped into and we can all benefit from that reminder."

— **CHUCK HOSKIN JR.**, *PRINCIPAL CHIEF, CHEROKEE NATION*

# 10 WAYS WE CAN ADVANCE SOCIAL JUSTICE

## WITHOUT DESTROYING EACH OTHER

HANNIBAL B. JOHNSON

BALKAN PRESS

# ACKNOWLEDGMENTS

"What is needed is a realization that power without love is reckless and abusive, and love without power is sentimental and anemic. Power at its best is love implementing the demands of justice, and justice at its best is love correcting everything that stands against love."[1]

— DR. MARTIN LUTHER KING, JR.

The author extends special thanks to the following individuals who provided invaluable feedback and assistance on various drafts of this work: William Bernhardt, Joseph Bojang, Richard DeSirey, Russ Florence, Sharon Gallagher, Randy Krehbiel, Kenneth J. Levit, Bill Major, Gary Percefull, Addie Richburg, Adam Simms, Wendy Thomas, Philip H. Viles, Jr., and Steve Wood.

# 10 Ways We Can Advance

# Social

# Justice

# Without Destroying Each Other

*Hannibal B. Johnson*

# TABLE OF CONTENTS

# WHAT IS SOCIAL JUSTICE?

## Social Justice is...

"**Social justice is** living in peace, with the equitable opportunity to flourish and thrive."

— *ALISON ANTHONY, PRESIDENT & CEO,*
*TULSA AREA UNITED WAY*

"**Social justice is** the full embodiment of the understanding that individuals in a community have a moral responsibility to openly and willingly uplift, defend, and care for one another."

— *PHIL ARMSTRONG, PRESIDENT & CEO,*
*OKLAHOMA CENTER FOR COMMUNITY AND*
*JUSTICE*

"**Social justice is** not Black justice. Social justice is not Christian justice. Social justice is for all freedom-loving people in the world. Social justice is a movement to uplift humanity itself."

— *FREEMAN CULVER, ED.D., PRESIDENT & CEO, GREENWOOD CHAMBER OF COMMERCE*

"**Social justice is** an active, intentional interruption of historical disenfranchisements so that commonly unheard or minimized voices or participants are engaged in meaningful, respectful ways—translating to access, opportunity, and equity."

— *DEWAYNE DICKENS, PH.D., DIRECTOR OF DIVERSITY, EQUITY, AND INCLUSION, TULSA COMMUNITY COLLEGE*

"**Social justice is** actively working to address and correct the impact of historical injustices and ensure our systems are equitable and just for all people."

— *MOISES ECHEVERRIA, PRESIDENT & CEO, FOUNDATION FOR TULSA SCHOOLS*

"**Social justice is** the work we do as humanity to be balanced and equitable in the treatment of others; the consideration and implementation of order and harmony to promote opportunity and a fair society in which all can thrive and function."

— *DAVID HARRIS, FORMER PRESIDENT, 100 BLACK MEN OF TULSA, INC.*

"**Social justice is** seeing the world through someone else's eyes and advocating for their experience."

— *TOBY JENKINS, FORMER CEO &*
*EXECUTIVE DIRECTOR, OKLAHOMANS FOR*
*EQUALITY*

"**Social justice is** the name we use to describe love in action among the human family as a whole. It is the embodiment of loving your neighbor. It is the truest expression of love of God."

— *REV. DR. MARLIN LAVANHAR, SENIOR*
*MINISTER, ALL SOULS UNITARIAN CHURCH*

"**Social justice is** equal access to goods, services, and resources for all, and not being treated with excessive scrutiny, punishment, or unnecessary penalties by the legal, financial, or political system in relation to others in our society."

— *SENATOR KEVIN L. MATTHEWS,*
*OKLAHOMA STATE SENATE*

"**Social justice is** making what's been denied, erased, hidden, and buried visible for all to see and then, once it's seen, we all have the responsibility to act."

— *ALICIA ODEWALE, PH.D., ASSISTANT*
*PROFESSOR OF ANTHROPOLOGY, UNIVERSITY*
*OF TULSA*

"**Social justice is** equitable access for all to the benefits that result from organizing ourselves into communities."

*— JOEY WIGNARAJAH, M.B.A., M.P.P.,*
*VENTURE CAPITALIST*

# Social Justice Icons

Dr. Ralph Abernathy * Kareem Abdul-Jabbar * Muhammad Ali * Susan B. Anthony * James Baldwin * Ida B. Wells Barnett * Harry Belafonte * Mary McLeod Bethune * Julian Bond * John Carlos * Cesar Chavez * Shirley Chisholm * Frederick Douglass * Dr. W.E.B. Du Bois * Medgar Evers * George Floyd * B.C. Franklin * RUTH BADER GINSBURG * Ada Lois Sipuel Fisher * Fannie Lou Hamer * Dorothy Height * Benjamin Hooks * Delores Huerta * LANGSTON HUGHES * Zora Neale Hurston * Jesse Jackson * Earvin "Magic" Johnson * Colin Kaepernick * Coretta Scott King * Dr. Martin Luther King, Jr. * Yuri Kochiyama * Fred Korematsu * John Lewis * Clara Luper * Chief Wilma Mankiller * Thurgood Marshall * Mamie Till Mobley * Rosa Parks * Sidney Poitier * Adam Clayton Powell, Jr. * A. Philip Randolph * Julius Rosenwald * Jackie Robinson * Eleanor Roosevelt * Bayard Rustin * Tommie Smith * A.J. Smitherman * Joel Elias Spingarn * Elizabeth Cady Stanton * Gloria Steinem * George Takei * Emmett Till * Harriet Tubman * Sojourner Truth * Booker T. Washington * Walter White * Richard Wright * Malcolm X * Whitney Young

# FOREWORD

## KENNETH J. LEVIT

"We have to speak up, we have to do the work, we have to organize other women to help us because we can't do it by ourselves. If all of us get together and put the pressure on our political leaders then we can make this happen."[1]

— DELORES HUERTA

This book is a wonderful primer for those interested in advancing social justice. It will inspire those not yet fully engaged in this task and reassure, reaffirm, and reinforce those already invested.

Johnson shares firsthand experiences and context-based insights from his decades of work and community-building around a host of social justice issues. His deep roots in diversity, equity, and inclusion ("DEI") work inform his approach, which centers on a basic notion of shared humanity.

He gifts us with a framework of 10 tactics for advancing social justice in our communities. The 10 constitute neither an exhaustive listing nor a sequential formula. Rather, Johnson presents 10 options for engagement, some of which will be better "fits" than others. The idea is to choose in accordance with one's proclivities and passions—to "get in where you fit in," choosing action over inaction.

Each chapter begins with an epigraph—a profound, provocative quote—and ends with "Framing Social Justice" and "Points to Ponder," further opportunities to explore, reflect on, and internalize the chapter's key elements.

If you want to grow in the realm of social justice—and I hope we all do—this book is for you. Whether you are a novice or a veteran, there is something here on which you can build.

A Scottish man named Nelson Henderson once said: "The true meaning of life is to plant trees, under whose shade you do not expect to sit." The work of social justice is the work of tree planting. And it's never too early or too late to start. Wherever you are in that cycle, Johnson's book will serve as a terrific guide.

# INTRODUCTION

"It is certain, in any case, that ignorance, allied with power, is the most ferocious enemy justice can have."[1]

— JAMES BALDWIN

"The arc of the moral universe is long, but it bends toward justice."[2]

— THEODORE PARKER

THE YEAR: 1977.
*Good Times. Happy Days. Charlie's Angels.*
Jimmy Carter. *Roots.* Disco.
The personal computer debuted. The death penalty reemerged. Snow fell in Miami.
And . . . a seventeen-year-old high school senior in Fort Smith, Arkansas, weary of perennial pennilessness, made an extraordinarily ordinary determination. The time had come for part-time work, after school and on weekends, to earn spending money.
Movies, fast food, clothes, football and basketball games:

teen indulgences don't pay for themselves. And $0.62/gallon gas, fuel for the mean, teen mobility machine—a classic 1963 Chevrolet Biscayne, black with mag wheels, vinyl upholstery, and fuzzy dice dangling from the rear-view mirror—was an essential expense, not a luxury.

This seemingly banal decision point proved anything but. The ultimate decider nixed the idea. The teen's father opposed on principle: "*School* is your job. It's full-time, and it demands your unwavering attention. If you need money, ask." No distractions. No diversions. No job.

The persistent high schooler and his strong-willed dad held firm to their respective convictions. Tensions mounted. Finally, after enduring his son's incessant pouting and plead-ing, the father relented. On condition that the boy maintain his near-perfect attendance and exceptional grades, the father blessed his son's search for a part-time job.

Through word-of-mouth, the determined teen learned of an opening for a stocker at a prominent drug store at the popular, centrally-located shopping mall, a veritable teen magnet. He decided to give it a go. He figured, "I'm pretty much the all-American teenager. I've got this."

The young man sported a stellar background, all reflected on his application, including: 4.00 grade point average—straight As, president of his high school senior class, all-state band member, and Boys State delegate. (American Legion Boys State is a highly respected and selective civic education summer camp for high school students.)

He submitted his application and was called for a personal interview. His time had come.

He prepared himself for the in-person exchange. Hair: check. Outfit: check. Confidence: check.

Though the butterflies fluttered, he felt assured of his ability to impress whatever adult might be on the other end of his employment equation. There was an impression to be made and he was ready to make it.

Showtime. The teen arrived at Central Mall, entered the store, and proceeded upstairs to the executive suite.

The store manager, a squat, middle-aged white man who seemed wholly unremarkable, greeted and seated him. With pleasantries aside, the interview commenced.

Avoiding the typical meandering trajectory of an adult-on-teen encounter, the interrogator cut to the chase. Looking the lad directly in the eyes, this all-too-officious-looking man muttered an obtuse admonition: "The last one we hired didn't work out."

A seemingly interminable pause followed. The sunny-spirited teen sat in a silent stupor, frozen momentarily by the icy insult (black ice—deadly but disguised). It reverberated. The last one we hired didn't work out. The last one we hired didn't work out. *The last one we hired didn't work out.*

"The last one" referred, unmistakably, to the last *Black* employee. The thinly veiled implication: "Even if I hire you, you will be watched. Your kind usually don't work out."

The prospective employer and his potential new hire, by some tacit, implicit agreement, proceeded with the session as though there had been no breach. Perhaps the manager genuinely believed that, but his interview subject felt vaguely violated and uncharacteristically impotent.

Standard questions followed: "When might you be available for work?" "Are there times when you absolutely cannot come in?" "Do you have reliable transportation?" There seemed to be a haze—a fog—that hovered over the remainder of the encounter.

The young man got the job. From the start, though, the manager habitually watched the neophyte from his upper chamber perch.

Two weeks in, the manager observed the teen visiting with some high school classmates while stocking shelves. That confirmed his bias. It proved enough evidence for termination, even though other employees routinely engaged with acquaintances who patronized the store. The manager saw this otherwise innocent, on-the-job banter with school friends as proof of the new hire's indolence. Bias confirmed. Prophecy fulfilled. Case closed.

The "why"—the rationale for the manager's decision—did not matter much. Had it not been this, it would have been that. The teen's fate had been foreshadowed; foreordained. As expected, he became the next "last one"—the cautionary tale; the proof in the pudding; the realization of someone else's self-fulfilling prophesy.

I was that teen. The encounter left me embarrassed, humiliated, and angry, yet, at seventeen, I lacked the wherewithal—the emotional intelligence—to respond as directly and candidly as I wish I had. Stunned silence was all that I could muster at the time.

*I was that teen.* Such was my first real, experiential, up-close-and-personal encounter with social *injustice*. My response, while woefully inadequate in retrospect, was as understandable then as it is regrettable now. Thankfully, I have since grown more astute, assured, and assertive.

The psychic pain from that experience, the first of several such incidents, lingers. Decades later, recalling that situation leads inexorably to a mental laundry list of unforgettable "You are Black and therefore . . ." moments—external reminders and cues that Blackness, in the minds of some, limits, constricts, and devalues.

I am not alone. That experience, *my experience*, is just a small part of a larger dynamic, systemic racism, which poses a real and present danger to the idea and ideal of social justice.

During the drug store interview, the manager spoke from a place of individual conviction and institutional (*i.e.*, systemic) power. His worldview, his not-uncommon conception of where Black people fit in his orbit, belonged not just to him as an individual, but to the store as an institution because of his position and power. His personal biases figured into his professional decision-making and shaped the culture of his workplace.

That manager's explicitly expressed implicit bias about Black people—*those* people—affected employment decisions about and life prospects for not just that one teen, but for the untold numbers of dark-skinned brothers and sisters with whom he dealt. The store, by elevating and empowering him with a leadership role, enabled and facilitated his prejudice.

That is but one small example of a theoretical and real phenomenon known as systemic racism. According to sociologist Joe R. Feagin:

> Systemic racism includes the complex array of anti-black practices, the unjustly gained political-economic power of whites, the continuing economic and other resource inequalities along racial lines, and the white racist ideologies and attitudes created to maintain and rationalize white privilege and power. *Systemic* here means that the core racist realities are manifested in each of society's major parts [...] each major part of U.S. society—the economy, politics, education, religion, the family—reflects the fundamental reality of systemic racism.[3]

Naming it allows us to address it. Acknowledgment is a necessary first step.

Theoretically, systemic racism is moored in the founding of the United States as a race-centric society, with Black people relegated to property status and racism embedded in social structures.[4] Practically, systemic racism today is evidenced by intersecting, overlapping, and co-dependent institutions, policies, practices, ideas, and behaviors that, wittingly and unwittingly, favor white people with resources, rights, and power that are denied to (or less accessible to) Black people and other people of color.

Consider our criminal justice system. Black people fare less well at virtually every stage of the game, from arrest, to prosecution, to adjudication, to sentencing. For a host of reasons, some complex and intricate, the criminal justice system, by many accounts, remains stacked against Black people.[5]

Yes, the blood, sweat, and tears of people of goodwill from all backgrounds have moved the needle on race and racism in this country. We are not where we once were.

We have made advances and inroads (though sometimes by taking two steps forward and one step back). We are better, but far from our best. Systemic racism remains one of many ills that stand in the way of social justice.

"Everything that has taken place in terms of creating change of a progressive nature involving race in America has been transactional.... Nothing in the area of social justice happens simply because it is morally correct, constitutionally appropriate or ethically right." So says Harry Edwards, Ph.D., sociologist, educator, professor emeritus at the University of California at Berkeley, and documentary film producer.[6]

We have all heard, and many of us have used, the term "social justice." What does it mean and how do we achieve it, transactionally or otherwise?

The concept of social justice can be traced back to 19th century disparities in wealth and social status reinforced by societal institutions. Fairness is key—fairness in individual-to-individual relations and fairness on an individual-to-society basis in terms of equitable access to wealth, opportunities, and social privileges. Core principles embedded in notions of social justice include access to resources, equity, participation, diversity, and human rights.[7]

Words typically associated with social justice include fairness, equity, equality, dignity, opportunity, economics, social, political, systems/systemic, institutions/institutional, community, and inclusion. All these words are related to the concept of shared humanity that lies at the core of our social justice concerns.

Our connectedness—our shared humanity—should be reason enough for us to relate to one another in ways that enhance, enliven, and enrich our lives; to gravitate toward a world in which social justice reigns supreme. Sadly, though, that is too infrequently the case. Social justice remains elusive. Creativity and consciousness-raising can speed up progress on the social justice front. So, too, can leading by example.[8]

Tulsa, Oklahoma, still grapples with the legacy of its defining disaster, the 1921 Tulsa Race Massacre, which destroyed the city's Black community, called the Greenwood District, and fondly dubbed "Black Wall Street" for its Black economic and entrepreneurial excellence.[9]

In the early 1900s, the Greenwood District, then often referred to as the "East End," teemed with entrepreneurial and business activity: doctors, lawyers, pharmacists, dentists, beauty parlors, barbershops, dance halls, pool halls, movie theaters, restaurants, and grocery stores. Greenwood Avenue, its nerve center, drew favorable comparisons to Beale Street in Memphis and State Street in Chicago.

The calamitous 1921 Tulsa Race Massacre, the worst of the 20th century "race riots," temporarily stilled the Greenwood District. Marauding rioters seized upon this segregated enclave, leaving in their wake death, destruction, and despair. It was the worst incident of mass racial violence against a Black community in United States history.

In a remarkable resurrection, the Greenwood District rose from the still-smoldering ashes, peaking in the 1940s. Beginning in the 1960s, changed social and economic conditions at the local, state, and national levels, integration and urban renewal chief among them, sparked a steep downward spiral.

Today, the Greenwood District is resurgent. The new Black Wall Street is a collaborative community consisting of residential, commercial, artistic, educational, cultural, entertainment, and religious elements working together to reclaim part of the past glory of this special, and for some, sacred, place.

Nonetheless, as a whole, Tulsa's Black residents are less well-off than white Tulsans on virtually every indicator of social, political, and economic well-being.[10] Gross racial disparities in education, health care, employment, and engagement in the criminal justice system are rooted in history. They derive in part from the structural, systemic, and institutional issues that spawned the Massacre and the subsequent decades-long failure to acknowledge, apologize, and atone for that monumental injustice.

Around the 100th anniversary of the Massacre (*i.e.*, May 31 – June 1, 2021), a Tulsa philanthropic entity launched a bold, multimillion-dollar initiative that reflects an evolution in philanthropic thinking. The aim was to empower historically underserved and underrepresented communities by directing attention and resources to self-identified needs.[11]

The Zarrow Families Foundation, originally established as a corporate charitable giving vehicle, morphed into a fund where brothers Henry and Jack Zarrow could do collaborative grantmaking outside their well-known individual foundations (*i.e.*, the Anne and Henry Zarrow Foundation and the Maxine and Jack Zarrow Family Foundation, respectively).

Zarrow Families Foundation trustees now direct grantmaking to support communities of color through the Zarrow Commemoration Fund. That Fund "support[s] bold and innovative efforts to correct social, political and economic injustices that impact [communities of color] in [the Tulsa] community." Its "grantmaking addresses disparities rooted in white supremacy and systemic racism with sustainable, collaborative solutions." I chair the Advisory Board of the Zarrow Commemoration Fund.

Bill Major, Executive Director of the various Zarrow entities,[12] noted:

Four basic tenets of social justice are equity, access, participation, and human rights. Through the Commemoration Fund, we (Zarrow Families Foundation) hoped to move beyond grantmaking directed to assist persons of color, to provide more equity, access, and participation. The best way we knew to do this was to give an Advisory Board, made up entirely of BIPOC [Black, Indigenous, and People of Color][13] individuals, the ability and the authority to make all the grantmaking decisions for the Fund. In this small way, we will inch towards a more just and equitable process and more grantmaking within a social justice context.[14]

In announcing the Zarrow Commemoration Fund, the Zarrow Families Foundation Trustees, Judy Zarrow Kishner, Gail Zarrow Richards, and Stuart Zarrow, noted: "We've decided to commit the funds of the entire joint family foundation to this cause. The Zarrow Families Foundation will now conduct its grantmaking through The Commemoration Fund, to honor the memory of the victims of the 1921 Tulsa Race Massacre. This new effort will be dedicated to and overseen entirely by people of color."[15]

Beginning with about $6 million, Advisory Board members award upwards of $1 million in community-based grants annually to projects that primarily serve the needs of people of color in the Tulsa area.[16]

The Zarrow Commemoration Fund elevates communities of color by: (1) empowering leaders of color in the ranks of philanthropy through service on its advisory board; (2) incentivizing nonprofits, through grantmaking criteria, to identify and develop people of color in their governance and management ranks; and (3) making seed funding available for nonprofits serving communities of color. It is an example of the "know, care, act" formula: *know* about a problem/issue; *care* about it and its consequences; *act* to intervene and improve the situation. Social justice changes are possible if we know, care, and act.

Social change is possible if we maintain hope in the face of the inevitable slings and arrows we face. As Jonas Salk counseled us: "Hope lies in dreams, in imagination, and in the courage of those who dare to make dreams into reality."

Hope is more than dreaming. Hope is the belief in one's capacity to fashion a brighter tomorrow. It is about ends, means, and one's capacity to connect them successfully—about goals, pathways, and agency.[17]

Ordinary people are capable of extraordinary things. Ordinary people helped found our nation, end slavery, silence Jim Crow, advance civil rights for Black Americans and other persons of color, promote women's rights, secure protections for the LBGTQ+ community, pass legislation supporting people with disabilities, champion First Amendment causes, preserve Native American sovereignty, push for immigration reform, address race-based health care disparities, and promote literacy and education. Ordinary people have been, are, and will be social justice lions.

Be extraordinarily ordinary. Seize the moment. Do the unimaginable.

## FRAMING SOCIAL JUSTICE

"There must exist a paradigm, a practical model for social change that includes an understanding of ways to transform consciousness that are linked to efforts to transform structures."[18]

— BELL HOOKS

# 1

## THE PILLARS OF SOCIAL JUSTICE: INTROSPECTION, ENGAGEMENT & ADVOCACY

"History, despite its wrenching pain cannot be unlived, but if faced with courage need not be lived again."[1]

— DR. MAYA ANGELOU

**social**
*adjective*
1. relating to society or its organization: "alcoholism is recognized as a major social problem"; *Similar* communal, community, community-based, collective, group

*Opposite:* individual

**justice**
*noun*
1. just behavior or treatment: "a concern for justice, peace, and genuine respect for people"; *Similar* fairness, justness, fair play, fair-mindedness, equity

*Opposite:* injustice[2]

THE THIRTY-FIRST PRESIDENT OF THE UNITED STATES, Herbert Clark Hoover, said: "Freedom is the open window through which pours the sunlight of the human spirit and human dignity." Calls for social justice remind us that Hoover's open window too often sports a screen that blocks rays emanating from the dispossessed and unfavored. Freedom allows the human spirit and human dignity to shine. Social justice allows them to penetrate.

Social justice matters because we—each of us—matter. Unless we learn to co-exist as equals, we will never live optimally. To denigrate any one of us is to demean all of us.

Absent the wholesale embrace of social justice, we risk succumbing to human tendencies to stereotype, "otherize," and scapegoat. Those tendencies, left unchecked, lead to horrific ends.

When we see ourselves in others, we understand that our shared humanity trumps all else. Through our disagreements, we must never doubt the dignity and worth of the other.

This book suggests 10 ways we can advance social justice —10 interventions or interrupters—cataloged at the end of this chapter and explored more fully in Chapter 5.

Between definition and intervention/interruption, however, it is critical to consider facts and factors that cause misalignments in the social order—inequality and inequity—social *injustice*.

We pay a cost for failing to internalize and act upon history's lessons. For example, our history teems with examples of fractious relations among racial, ethnic, and cultural groups and an overarching white supremacist ideology that places some at an advantage at the expense of others. Recognizing our shared humanity—and the power of "we"—and rectifying disparities and inequities are among the chief aims of social justice initiatives.

Through critical thinking, we best position ourselves to tackle seemingly overwhelming social justice issues. We can begin to address: mass incarceration, sexual violence, religious discrimination, the school-to-prison pipeline, gun violence, book-banning, and censorship[3]; the wealth gap, voting rights, environmental degradation/climate change, hunger/food insecurity, healthcare disparities, educational inequities, employment discrimination, community/police dynamics, discrimination and violence targeting the LGBTQ+ community, colorism, gender equity, racial/ethnic discrimination, and hate crimes; immigration and historical reckoning, including reparations.

To be ready, we must know, care, and act: *know*—look at ourselves, others, events, and institutions; *care*—reflect on recurring inequalities and inequities; and *act*—work on solutions to effect and advance meaningful, measurable, maintainable solutions.

Critical thinking animates the three core activities necessary for social justice advancement: (1) introspection; (2) engagement; and (3) advocacy.

**Introspection**

The examination or observation of one's own mental and emotional processes: "Quiet ***introspection***—self-reflection— can be of enormous value."

*Introspection is self-examination—looking at oneself through clear, distortion-free lenses with a view toward honestly assessing one's full self and, where appropriate, taking corrective action.*

**Engagement**

The action of engaging or being engaged: "The United States' continued ***engagement*** with NATO has borne political and economic fruit."

*Engagement is plugging into the community in ways that ignite one's passions and align with one's values.*

## Advocacy

Public support for, or recommendation of, a particular cause or policy: "The agency's *advocacy* of criminal justice reform led to changes within the police department."

*Advocacy is publicly promoting, catalyzing, and mobilizing people and resources around issues and causes one supports.*

These abstract concepts—introspection, engagement, and advocacy—have practical application. One example comes immediately to mind.

A summer youth camp I directed for fifteen years, Anytown, Oklahoma (now known as the Anytown Leadership Institute), attests to the power of this three-part model. Anytown, still an ongoing flagship program of the Oklahoma Center for Community and Justice (OCCJ), is a week-long, residential, leadership and human relations camp for high school sophomores, juniors, and seniors that promotes self-esteem, citizenship, and social justice in a diverse environment. This summer youth diversity leadership camp, modeled on a program that debuted in Arizona in 1957, encourages introspection, engagement, and advocacy in service of our shared humanity.

The Anytown journey traverses vast but interconnected subject matter terrain: developing leadership skills, honing interpersonal communication skills, engendering multicultural awareness, promoting interreligious understanding, examining individual and systemic discrimination, and addressing prejudice and discrimination.

Anytown teaches young people to overcome biases and other challenges by instilling a sense of self-worth. It fosters meaningful interaction among youth of various backgrounds. It cultivates usable skills that enable young people to create positive change in their own actions and attitudes and become change agents in their own environments.

Anytowners learn about the effects of prejudice and discrimination. They develop positive self-esteem and burnish their leadership skills. They enhance their citizenship skills and capacities.[4] In sum, Anytown prepares young people for the diverse, interconnected, complex world in which they live.

In my role as camp director, I set the tone for the experience at the outset with a simple but profound assurance: "You may not always feel comfortable, but you should always feel safe." That mantra bears repeating as we grapple with the myriad social justice issues confronting us. There will be moments of discomfort, no doubt. But if we fully embrace our shared humanity, then we can navigate the discomfort without fear of reprisal.

Staff assign teens attending Anytown, known as "delegates," to gender-aligned cabins. College-age counselors supervise the cabins. Prior to camp, counselors, all former Anytown delegates, undergo training in group dynamics, conflict resolution, and diversity leadership. The adults who supervise the program, called "advisors," also participate in this training.

Like the delegates themselves, both counselors and advisors reflect the rich diversity of the state and nation, not just in terms of race, but also the many other dimensions of diversity (e.g., ethnicity, gender, gender identity, sexual orientation, culture, religion, economic status, and political affiliation) and the intersectionality (i.e., the web of diversities within a single individual) to which so many people can relate.

Discussion groups led by counselors and advisors meet daily to discuss the assigned themes and other topics. Workshops by advisors and invited guests cover a broad base of concerns and issues.

Anytowners explore systems of oppression, including racism, sexism, homophobia, and classism, in a non-judgmental environment that encourages critical thinking. They learn about culture and religion. Many explore, for the first time, their own cultural identity and background.

Through it all, they connect with their own innate capacities for compassion and empathy. They discover the common ground that is our shared humanity.

Each day at Anytown centers around a theme that builds progressively toward the theme of inclusion and shared humanity: Get Acquainted; Know Yourself; Know Your Family; Know Your Friends; Know Your Community; and After Anytown.

Think of the "Know Yourself" theme as equivalent to introspection. Think of "Know Your Family," "Know Your Friends," and "Know Your Community" as part of an engagement process. View "After Anytown" as advocacy, posing the question, "Now that I know these things, what am I going to do to further the message of inclusion and shared humanity?"

The Anytown theme song, sung reluctantly on day one and with gusto on day six, captures the inclusive vibe that pervades the experience:

*CHORUS*
**Anytown, Anytown;**
**People of all colors and all backgrounds.**
**Makes no difference when you**
**come down**
**To Anytown, our Anytown.**
*An outstretched hand, a friendly face,*
*From another creed, another race;*
*These are things we have by grace,*
*At Anytown, our Anytown.*
***[Chorus]***
*Sometimes people just don't bother,*
*Care for themselves, never for others;*

*We can show them we're sisters and brothers,*
*At Anytown, our Anytown.*
**[Chorus]**
*If you listen, you can hear it,*
*What we call THE ANYTOWN SPIRIT!;*
*Love for others will bring you near it,*
*At Anytown, our Anytown.*
**[Chorus]**

Likewise, a nightly closing circle at Anytown offers students (delegates) an opportunity for sharing reflections on the day: *How did you feel about what you experienced? What insights did you gain from the day? What did you realize about yourself and others based on the day's activities?* The circle is a sacred symbol, representing wholeness, infinity, totality, and divinity. At Anytown, the circle stands for equality, interdependence, and mutual respect—for the power of "we."

Anytown helps teens appreciate the richness of their own culture and heritage and enhance their capacity to respect and honor the culture and heritage of others. It demonstrates, through experiential immersion, that the connections we share as human beings run deeper than our differences.

Julian Thomas, a former Anytown delegate, counselor, and advisor, now an accomplished New York actor, shared a 2002 experience illustrative of the possibilities borne of such a welcoming, nurturing, inclusive environment.

I can recall during an evening presentation on race relations, a young brother who fell suddenly despondent in the room. Simply walking over to him and asking the young man to step outside with me seemed a small enough gesture at the time. Besides, there was only a handful of African-American males on staff—not to mention the camp director—and I saw it more as providence than an obligation. It only took a minute or two of silence, leaned over on a porch stoop for him to start talking, and I relished the opportunity to listen . . .

An incident, not gang related, had broken out just the night before between the young man's older brother and members from a rival school. His brother was shot and killed, he lamented, and he was simply glad to be at camp, away from it all. He finished the story by remarking that if he wasn't out here 'in the middle of God knows where,' he would most certainly have found his brother's killer and retaliated himself.

Sometimes there is nothing more to do or say than to listen and offer a shoulder to cry on. That is exactly what I did that day and I hope the experience remains with me forever.[5]

Anytown profoundly impacts every Oklahoma teen who attends. It transforms staff, too. Anytown changes lives.

Former Anytown delegates, in their own words, said it best. One enthused: "This total experience has enlightened my life." Yet another gushed: "I really want to share this experience with as many people as I can. I've never had this much fun while learning so much." Two others raved: "This has been the best week of my life. Thanks, Anytown!" and "These experiences, times, and people are the best of my life."[6]

The former President and CEO of the nonprofit that runs Anytown, OCCJ, is himself an Anytown alumnus.

Moises Echeverria arrived in Tulsa, Oklahoma, as a thirteen-year-old Spanish-speaking middle school student. His family immigrated from Monterrey, Mexico. He faced the challenge of learning a new language and adapting to a new culture.[7]

Fast forward four years. A high school counselor extended an invitation to this reserved and still-acclimating seventeen-year-old. Moises accepted the invitation and embarked upon an experience that would change his life trajectory.

His world expanded. He blossomed. He began a two-decade relationship with OCCJ. After Anytown, Moises engaged more deeply with OCCJ and school clubs. He accepted the role of student representative on the OCCJ board of directors. He served as an Anytown counselor for several years. Following graduation from Oklahoma State University, Moises continued to volunteer for OCCJ, and ultimately joined the organization as its program coordinator. In November 2016, he became President and CEO.[8]

Anytown is a microcosm of what might be in the real world if we focused intently on living, learning, and growing together. One Anytown alumnus observed, "Once your eyes have been opened, it is impossible to shut them again." To see and hear other perspectives—to walk a mile in the shoes of the other—helps to understand and, it is hoped, accept, our individual and collective responsibility to social justice.

Another example of connecting youth with their own agency around social justice is Tulsa Changemakers,[9] the brainchild of two Teach For America Tulsa transplants, Andrew Spector from Bedford, Massachusetts,[10] and Jake Lerner from Philadelphia, Pennsylvania.[11]

Tulsa Changemakers empowers promising youth leaders to drive positive impact in Tulsa now and into the future. It imagines Tulsa as a model city for youth-driven impact—a place where youth are core catalysts for impact in their community, and the community is actively engaged in identifying, developing, and empowering youth as leaders. Tulsa Changemakers wants Tulsa to be a city that consistently cultivates highly effective community leaders eager to empower successive generations.

Through after-school and out-of-school leadership development and community engagement programming for students, and via training and consulting with and for adults,

Tulsa Changemakers casts youth as instruments of social justice.

The Tulsa Changemakers co-founders see the program as a force multiplier.

> Tulsa Changemakers is a force for social justice not only because the community impact initiatives of the young people align with broader social justice movements, [but also because] the very engagement of young people in this way is an act of social justice. We are cultivating agency in young people, primarily youth of color from low-income communities, and positioning them as active and powerful stewards of their lives, schools, and communities, not as obstacles or passive recipients.
>
> In doing so, youth are multiplying their impact by becoming catalysts for the adults in their lives to join them in their efforts. Ultimately, long-term change will be made possible because those closest to the challenges are the best positioned to identify and drive the solutions. [12]

A Tulsa Changemakers summer program bears witness. "Power of Youth," billed as a crash course in how to show up for your community, debuted in 2022. Aimed at students in grades six through twelve, the free, six-session facilitated program tackled topics like "Levers of Power," "The Power of Public Speaking," "The Power of Petitioning," "The Power of Innovation," and "The Power of Protest," and then culminated in a session centered on "Reflection and Power Mapping." [13]

Anytown and Tulsa Changemakers demonstrate the capacity of youth to embrace and embody social justice. How might we do the same?

Once again, consider the three pillars—introspection, engagement, and advocacy—from an individual perspective.

How does one honor them in ways that promote social justice —ways that foster DEI?

DEI envisions a just society in which our shared humanity is the supreme value, opportunity exists for all irrespective of our various differences, and fairness is the watchword. Within the DEI framework, social justice looks more intently at gaps in the ideal state—at instances in which we are not living up to our ideals—with a view toward narrowing, and ultimately, eliminating gulfs of injustice.[14]

At the individual level, I might, upon reflection, conclude a more expansive circle of relationships would further my desire to fully embrace DEI. I might identify, prioritize, and target the relationships I need to build to grow in the realm of DEI. (*Introspection*)

I might then seek out and work with organizations whose missions center on bringing people together, facilitating dialogue, and bridging divides in my community. I might commit my time (*e.g.*, volunteering), talent (*e.g.*, serving on a governance board), or treasure (*e.g.*, making a financial contri-bution) to such organizations. (*Engagement*)

I might also, through those organizations or otherwise, closely monitor practices, policies, and laws that affect DEI matters. To narrow gaps in practices, policies, and laws that adversely affect equity, I might more carefully consider my voting to support candidates at all levels who back DEI-friendly practices, policies, and laws. I might engage in educa-tional and/or lobbying efforts that support culturally compe-tent curricula and inclusive educational initiatives. (*Advocacy*)

Many organizations explicitly commit to social justice as part of their mission or in a separate pledge. One such pledge from the University of Pittsburgh School of Public Health illustrates the profound power of possibilities borne of full inclusion.

## PLEDGE TO SOCIAL JUSTICE AND ANTIRACISM

> The Department of Environmental and Occupational Health...calls out structural racism as a chronic public health malady. Environmental racism and injustice persist with marginalized communities experiencing disproportionate exposure to hazardous waste, air pollutants, and toxic chemicals. We will work to empower all people to live free from environmental stressors that adversely affect human health. We acknowledge [our] racist past. Our departmental demographics (faculty, students and staff) lacks diversity. We hereby pledge to be Antiracist in our educational programs, research, and practice.[15]

In furtherance of its social justice and antiracism pledge, the Department cited specific DEI initiatives it would undertake; among them, increasing campus diversity, fostering a supportive and nurturing learning environment, encouraging civil discourse, and dismantling systemic inequities.[16]

Agents for social justice must stay "woke," in the original sense of the term, which emanates from Black American English vernacular, meaning: "to be aware of and actively attentive to important issues (especially issues of racial and social justice)."[17] "Wokeness," as coined and contemplated by the Black community, suggests an awakening, an enlightenment, to the workings of the world—to the ways in which structures, institutions, and systems work for, and in too many cases, against, segments of society. Wokeness—this penchant for identifying and calling out inequities—thus threatens the status quo, the powerful and the privileged.

In what might be described as cultural misappropriation, some have twisted "woke" and "wokeness" into negatives— snarky references, often in the context of performative antics to an imagined hypersensitivity to social issues, particularly those plaguing persons of color and other marginalized groups (*e.g.*, women, LGBTQ+ persons, immigrants).[18] The racialized dynamic inherent in this commandeering of language is inescapable.

That said, to be "woke" is not to be anti-white—indeed, it is not to be *anti*-anything. Quite the contrary, to be woke is to be fully attuned to our shared humanity; staunchly committed to inclusion; and profoundly motivated to act in ways that fulfill the promise of our Union: *E pluribus unum* (a Latin phrase meaning "out of many, one").

That unity credo, our professed understanding of our shared humanity, must be constantly reinforced. Our history suggests the promotion of a racial pecking order damages the psyche of both the powerful and the put-upon; the dominant and the dispossessed; the oppressors and the oppressed.

Scientific genius and humanitarian Dr. Albert Einstein understood the importance of racial justice. He corresponded with Black intellectual Dr. W.E.B. Du Bois about the status of Black Americans. He bemoaned the struggle for social justice on matters of race and urged support for Black empowerment.[19]

Our shared humanity should animate our desire to work for social justice.[20] Failing that, our own self-interest, both individual and collective, should suggest to us that the long road toward social justice is the prudent path forward— indeed, it is the *only* viable path forward.

Following are 10 ways to help us navigate that path—10 ways we can advance social justice.

## 10 Ways We Can Advance Social Justice

1. **Speak truth.**
2. **Listen intently.**
3. **Show up.**
4. **Engage with your community.**

5. **Seek to serve.**
6. **Align with allies.**
7. **Play politics.**
8. **Delve into Diversity, Equity & Inclusion.**
9. **Pledge allegiance.**
10. **Walk the walk.**[21]

---

**FRAMING SOCIAL JUSTICE**

---

"And I must say tonight that a riot is the language of the unheard. And what is it America has failed to hear? It has failed to hear that the promises of freedom and justice have not been met. And it has failed to hear that large segments of white society are more concerned about tranquility and the status quo than about justice and humanity."[22]

— DR. MARTIN LUTHER KING, JR.

## Points to Ponder

Who are you from a social justice perspective?
**(Introspection)**

How are you plugged into your community?
**(Engagement)**

For what are you willing to stand—to sacrifice?
**(Advocacy)**

## 2

# PLANNING FOR SOCIAL JUSTICE

"There are two ways of exerting one's strength: one is pushing down; the other is pulling up."[1]

— BOOKER T. WASHINGTON

THE UNITED NATIONS GENERAL ASSEMBLY, BY RESOLUTION dated November 26, 2007, recognized a "World Day of Social Justice" that has been celebrated since 2009.[2] In context, "Social justice is about fairness. It encompasses basic needs, opportunities, wealth, and every other system within society. Closely aligned with human rights, social justice is about ensuring equality for all people."[3]

The late Filipino Justice Jose P. Laurel offered a compelling, rather academic, definition of social justice.

Social justice means the promotion of the welfare of all the people, the adoption by the Government of measures calculated to insure economic stability of all the component elements of society, through the maintenance of a proper economic and social equilibrium in the interactions of the members of the community, constitutionally, through the adoption of measures legally justifiable, or extra-constitutionally through the exercise of powers underlying the existence of all Governments on the time-honored principle of *Salus Populi est suprema lex.* ["The safety of the people is the supreme law."][4]

A more practical definition of social justice emphasizes fairness in relations between individuals in society and equal access to wealth, opportunities, and social privileges. Five key principles lie at its core: access to resources, equity, participation, diversity, and human rights.[5]

Under both the academic and the practical definitions, the goal of social justice is a society in which all individuals have equitable access to resources and receive equitable treatment. This idealized outcome is wholly consistent with the logical extension of sentiments boldly expressed in the Preamble to the Declaration of Independence: "We hold these truths to be self-evident, that all men are created equal, that they are endowed by their Creator with certain unalienable Rights, that among these are Life, Liberty and the pursuit of Happiness."[6]

Dimensions of diversity—*e.g.*, race, ethnicity, national origin, gender, gender identity and expression, religion, ability status—reflect facets of who we are, and should be acknowledged and respected accordingly. They should not be cause for negative treatment; for social *injustice*.

Stated differently, the aim of this work is the "beloved community[7]," which comes into being "when people of diverse racial, ethnic, educational, class, gender, abilities, sexual orientation backgrounds/identities come together in an interdependent relationship of love, mutual respect, and care that seeks to realize justice within the community and in the broader world."[8] Getting there—realizing social justice and achieving something approaching the beloved community—requires that we know, care, and act: that we *know*—appreciate the importance of equality and equity; that we *care*—show concern for disparities and inequities; and that we *act*—take appropriate remedial action.

For some, the longing for the beloved community took on additional meaning and urgency following the January 6, 2021, insurrection.[9] Cracks in our democracy, an implicit foundational element underlying the beloved community and, arguably, essential to social justice, became apparent. These chinks in our democratic armor were rooted in dual lies: (1) the existence of widespread election fraud; and (2) the imperative of white supremacy, as evidenced by the rise of white nationalism and the increasingly prevalent "great replacement theory" rhetoric.

The antidemocratic violence we witnessed on January 6, 2021, and the spoken and unspoken sentiments undergirding it revealed and perhaps widened a great national abyss. Calls for a beloved community *plus*—for a 21st century Great Society initiative—rang out.

> [A] reinvigorated vision of a more inclusive democracy… means expanding and protecting access to voting, creating legislation to protect people who face discrimination, promoting civics education and teaching students an anti-racist curriculum, and ensuring all Americans have healthcare, housing and other vital services so they can lead safe and dignified lives.[10]

The quest for social justice involves both the individual and the collective: "Right attitudes are never sufficient alone. They must find embodiment in social institutions. Indeed, one must say that one does not even understand the meaning of 'right attitudes' or even of a theology until one recognizes their implications for social organization."[11]

Initial steps on the collective journey to the aspirational beloved community (or beloved community *plus*) include facilitating constructive conversations about social justice issues that empower those engaged in the dialogue and provoke critical thinking around personal and societal remedies.

Following are important questions to consider when evaluating and planning around social justice issues:

- **Who makes decisions and who is left out (presently and/or historically) of the decision-making process?** Representation— *active, non-token* representation—matters. Diverse voices round out the chorus and make its selections rich and robust. When in the decision-making arena, see those seated around the table, but also envision those who do not occupy seats: who is present, and who is missing.

- **Who benefits from and who endures the consequences of decisions?** Consider who benefits from and who is burdened by a particular decision (*e.g.*, law, rule, or policy). Think about the choices being made and the resultant consequences those choices yield.

- **Why is a given law, rule, policy, practice, or other measure fair or unfair?** Consider both the intention and the impact of any given measure. Ask whether a given law, rule, policy, practice, or other measure is equitable—fair to all. Think about what might be done to equitably apportion benefits and burdens.

- **What is required to create durable change (*e.g.*, policy shifts, allies)?** Change, while always possible, may not be easy. Find the locus of power and leverage relationships in ways that move power in the direction of the desired changes. Demonstrate that change in the direction of equity serves the long-term interests of all.

- **What are our individual and collective roles in facilitating any necessary change?** Change comes not through magic, but through the affirmative efforts of committed people. Change agents, not change advocates, get things done.

- **What alternative outcomes might we imagine as the result of our efforts?** Play out the various scenarios that might come to fruition, from no change to the achievement of the desired outcome and everything in between. Envision the possibilities and shape them through your actions.

- **How do we define "success"?** Imagine "winning" and describe what you see. Watch for wins. Mark milestones. Celebrate incremental victories. Complete and total success may never be achieved. Even if it is, it may be long in coming and short in duration. Define success so that both the path toward it and its achievement and maintenance become clear.

- **What steps might we take to ensure any changes are sustainable?** Achieving success does not guarantee maintaining and sustaining it. Plan for sustaining success over the long term.[12]

## FRAMING SOCIAL JUSTICE

"Prisons do not disappear social problems, they disappear human beings. Homelessness, unemployment, drug addiction, mental illness, and illiteracy are only a few of the problems that disappear from public view when the human beings contending with them are relegated to cages."[13]

— ANGELA DAVIS

### POINTS TO PONDER

On which social justice issue(s) are you willing to go all in?

Who are your natural allies as you tackle these social justice issues?

How will you lead or participate in the planning process that results in an effective, sustainable strategy to address the social justice issue(s)?

# 3

## SEEKING SOCIAL JUSTICE: A STRATEGIC APPROACH

"The challenge of social justice is to evoke a sense of community that we need to make our nation a better place, just as we make it a safer place."[1]

— MARIAN WRIGHT EDELMAN

SEEKING SOCIAL JUSTICE (AT LEAST *EFFECTIVELY* SEEKING social justice), like most other pursuits, benefits from strategic planning. Social justice issues are nettlesome and entrenched —systemic. An *ad hoc*, seat-of-the-pants approach is likely to frustrate and fail. A structured approach increases the probability of sound, lasting solutions.

To be clear, not all meaningful change happens in a structured context. Structure, though, enhances prospects for deep, durable penetration—for sustainable change.

Consider the following strategy,[2] more fully discussed later, for addressing social justice issues:

(1) Establish rules of engagement for social justice conversations (by consensus, where possible).

(2) Capture the context. Engage participants around DEI to ground them in the structural, institutional, and systemic bases of the social justice issues that need to be addressed.[3]

(3) Clarify the social justice challenge at hand using the "IRAC" paradigm:

- "**I**"—Define the central **issue(s)**;
- "**R**"—Identify the **rules**, standards, and practices relevant to the issue(s);
- "**A**"—Conduct an **analysis** of the interrelationship between the rules, standards, and practices relevant to the issue(s); and
- "**C**"—Draw **conclusions** that point to interventions needed to improve the issue(s).

(4) Immerse yourself in the history of the social justice issue(s) under consideration: How did we get to where we are today?

(5) Consider ways to engage—to involve a diverse audience in multiple, meaningful ways—around the social justice issue(s).

(6) Identify existing and prospective allies.

(7) Develop a systematic approach to addressing the social justice issue(s) (*i.e.*, goals, timelines, responsible parties, and milestones).

(8) Define success: What does it look like and how will it be measured, qualitatively and quantitatively?

Now, take a closer look at each of the foregoing steps in this strategy for addressing social justice issues.

## 1. Establish rules of engagement for social justice conversations.

What are the norms that lay a foundation for thoughtful, respectful, constructive dialogue? These critical boundaries prove particularly invaluable when discussing social justice issues involving race, racism, and racial violence, all of which are fraught with emotion, pain, and trauma.

The following four agreements for courageous conversations encourage open, forthright, robust dialogue:

- **Stay engaged**: Listen actively; share generously; and think critically.
- **Speak your truth**: Own your experiences, observations, and perceptions; let others own theirs. Use "I" messages. Your truth is the only truth to which you can authoritatively speak.
- **Experience discomfort**: You may not always feel comfortable, but you should always feel safe. Temporary discomfort borne of inconvenient truths and a painful past is a necessary steppingstone to progress.
- **Expect and accept non-closure**: The difficult social justice issues at the crux of social justice challenges are ongoing—chronic. A social justice conversation, however robust, cannot solve all the world's problems, but it can begin to acknowledge, articulate, and analyze some of them.[4]

Five values—R.O.P.E.S., for short—support the four agreements: Respect, Openness, Participation, Energy, and Sensitivity.

This four-by-five formulation—the four agreements plus the five values—establishes sound rules of engagement for most social justice conversations.

## 2. Capture the context.

Context is key. As such, this second element of the social justice strategy—capture the context—merits additional breadth and depth. DEI is the context—the environmental backdrop—for social justice issues.

The next chapter takes a closer look at DEI. It defines critical DEI terms, makes the case for DEI, relates examples of DEI in action, and examines some of our DEI baggage.

DEI rests upon a foundation of shared humanity. That is, DEI emphasizes the dignity and worth of each of us. If DEI were the North Star of social interaction and engagement, accepted and embraced by all, social justice issues would dissipate and, in a perfect world, disappear.

## 3. Clarify the social justice challenge(s) at hand.

Use the "IRAC" paradigm, a popular law school hypothetical issue-spotting stratagem, to define the particular social justice challenge (*i.e.*, **I**ssue(s), **R**ule(s), **A**nalysis, and **C**onclusion(s)): "**I**"—Define the central issue(s); "**R**"—Identify the rules, standards, and practices relevant to the issue(s); "**A**"—Analyze the interrelationship between the rules, standards, and practices relevant to the issue(s); and "**C**"—Draw conclusions that suggest interventions needed to improve the issue(s).

This framing crystallizes the issues and illuminates the steps needed for corrective action.

Consider the emergence of Black Lives Matter ("BLM")[5], founded to address the core issue of the killings of unarmed Black men by law enforcement officers (the issue; "I" ). Its official mission:

#BlackLivesMatter was founded in 2013 in response to the acquittal of Trayvon Martin's murderer. Black Lives Matter Global Network Foundation, Inc. is a global organization in the US, UK, and Canada, whose mission is to eradicate white supremacy and build local power to intervene in violence inflicted on Black communities by the state and vigilantes. By combating and countering acts of violence, creating space for Black imagination and innovation, and centering Black joy, we are winning immediate improvements in our lives.[6]

The rules, standards, and practices applicable to the killings of unarmed young Black men (and some women) by law enforcement include criminal laws, police practices, and the inner-workings of the criminal justice system (*e.g.*, the jury selection process). None of these explicitly justify such killings. Though these rules, standards, and practices are facially neutral (*i.e.*, they do not appear, on the surface, to be discriminatory), they play out in ways BLM and many others consider unjust (the rules; "R").

Something about these rules, standards, and practices as applied in the context of the criminal justice system creates inequity (the analysis; "A"). That "something" may include systemic racism, implicit bias, and structural issues in the law and within the criminal justice system.

As such, BLM works to shed light on the issues, reform law enforcement agencies, and advocate for remedial legislation (the conclusion; "C").

### 4. Immerse yourself in the history of the social justice issue(s) under consideration.

How did we get to where we are today?

"We learn from history that we do not learn from history." Georg Wilhelm Friedrich Hegel got it right: We humans are not inclined to internalize the lessons of our past. As such, we are destined to repeat our mistakes.

Knowing the history surrounding a given social justice issue enables us to see it for what it is and attack it at its roots.

## 5. Consider ways to engage around the social justice issue(s) under consideration.

Social justice issues often seem overwhelming—mammoth, colossal, gargantuan. It is difficult to step into a breach with seemingly no chance of fully closing the gap. We are too often intimidated into inaction.

In the social justice arena, incremental change should be welcomed, too. Individual efforts, collectively considered, can make meaningful change.

Tennis legend and humanitarian Arthur Ashe is credited with saying: "Start where you are. Use what you have. Do what you can." That is a powerful formula for stimulating engagement around social justice issues.

## 6. Identify existing and potential allies.

Who might you actively cultivate as allies?

Allies are critical—people with whom we may not share identities and direct experiences, but who exhibit compassion and empathy; people who willingly put themselves at personal risk for us and our cause(s).

In race matters, for example, white allies, and particularly, white Jewish allies, have long played important roles.

The NAACP, the National Association for the Advancement of Colored People, one of the nation's leading civil rights organizations, began in 1909 as an interracial organization. Black civil rights were its focus, but leaders understood that achievement of the NAACP's aims required inputs from those outside the Black community.

Among its early leaders was Joel Spingarn, a Jewish intellectual and racial justice advocate who served as chairman of the NAACP board of directors (1913 – 1919), treasurer (1919 - 1930), and second president (1930 – 1939). In 1914, Joel Spingarn established the Spingarn Medal, which is awarded annually by the NAACP to an African American for his/her outstanding achievement. The Spingarn Medal continues the Black-Jewish allyship in perpetuity.

**7. Develop a strategic approach to addressing social justice issue(s) (*i.e.*, goals, timelines, responsible parties, and milestones).**

"If you fail to plan, you are planning to fail." Benjamin Franklin spoke truth centuries ago. In social justice matters, planning counts. Look no further than the Civil Rights Movement of the 1950s and 1960s for evidence of extensive strategic planning to social justice ends.

We sometimes oversimplify social justice concerns. We think, "If everyone would be compassionate and considerate, our problems would abate." Our essential social justice challenges, though, operate on systemic, structural, and institutional levels, too. We have to plan accordingly—beyond the "be nice" level. "[K]indness alone rarely brings about change. Change requires a real understanding of what injustice looks like—and a plan to combat it."[7]

**8. Define success: What does success look like and how will it be measured, qualitatively and quantitatively?**

Begin with an end in mind. What do we want? How will we know if we have gotten it? How do we hold on to the advances we make? Answering these key questions requires evaluation and measurement.

---
**FRAMING SOCIAL JUSTICE**

---

"Equality of opportunity is not enough. Unless we create an environment where everyone is guaranteed some minimum capabilities through some guarantee of minimum income, education, and healthcare, we cannot say that we have fair competition. When some people have to run a 100-meter race with sandbags on their legs, the fact that no one is allowed to have a head start does not make the race fair. Equality of opportunity is absolutely necessary but not sufficient in building a genuinely fair and efficient society."[8]

— HA-JOON CHANG

## Points to Ponder

How will you evaluate the social justice planning process?

What criteria define success in social justice planning?

Who is responsible for implementing the social justice plan?

## 4

## SOCIAL JUSTICE AND DIVERSITY, EQUITY & INCLUSION

"Unity, not uniformity, must be our aim. We attain unity only through variety. Differences must be integrated, not annihilated, not absorbed."[1]

— MARY PARKER FOLLETT

ACHIEVING SOCIAL JUSTICE IS THE WORK OF DEI. THAT IS, valuing diversity, achieving equity, and embracing inclusion are the essential pillars that undergird social justice. As such, an understanding of the fundamentals of DEI is critical.

### Diversity, Equity & Inclusion

Three key words, "diversity," "equity," and "inclusion," merit further reflection.

Diversity refers to the many and varied differences among us, some often apparent (*e.g.*, gender or race) and some often not (*e.g.*, learning styles or economic status). These differences are set against an overarching commonality: our shared humanity.

Equity (*i.e.*, fairness) is central to inclusion. In fact, DI (diversity and inclusion), rather than DEI (diversity, equity, and inclusion), was once the more widely-used label for conversations about human differences. Inclusion implies equity, but many felt it important to call out equity explicitly.

Equity involves trying to understand and give people *what they need* to enjoy their full humanity. Equality, by contrast, aims to ensure that everyone gets the same things to enjoy their full humanity.

Both equality and equity aim to promote fairness and justice, but a fixation on equality achieves these ideals only if everyone starts from the same place and needs the same things.

We do not all start from the same place. We do not all need the same things. Geneticists and historians concur on this point. A singular focus on equality, then, comes up short in terms of optimizing fairness and justice.

Equity, a critical component of inclusion, requires a recognition of individual circumstances and a steadfast commitment to individual excellence. Paired with aspirational equality, equity gets us closer to the fairness and justice we seek.

The following graphic illustrates the point:

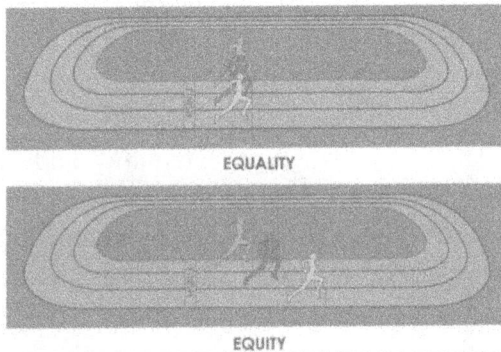

EQUALITY

EQUITY

The foregoing image[2] depicts runners on an oval racetrack. The outer lanes of the track are longer than the inner ones. If all runners started at the same place (*i.e.*, equality), some runners would have to run farther than others to reach the finish line. They would be disadvantaged from the start, as are people who are subjected to systemic oppression. If, however, the runners begin at various places along the track to compensate for the varying distances of the assigned lanes (*i.e.*, equity), we build in fundamental fairness—we compensate for the disadvantage built into the track.[3]

Inclusion, the welcome and full recognition of the humanity of others, demands both equal access and consideration of history—history that leaves some disadvantaged from the start.

Inclusion comes with the recognition that what we as people have in common far exceeds our differences. Inclusion is a state of being respected, valued, and supported within a community such that each person is given the opportunity to reach full potential.

Hallmarks of inclusion include feeling welcome, secure, safe, engaged, respected, heard, connected, empowered, valued, and appreciated.

Diversity is. Inclusion (and with it, equity) may or may not be. In other words, diversity already exists. Inclusion has to be cultivated.

Diversity is who we already are demographically. We are of various races, ethnicities, genders, gender identities, sexual orientations, and abilities. We are different—diverse—in many other ways.

Inclusion depends on consciousness and affirmative action in terms of how we embrace diversity. Inclusion is a matter of how we act upon our differences; how we accommodate the needs of the many in service of the whole and in recognition of our shared humanity.

## Intersectionality

Race is but one of the many dimensions of diversity, some internal, some external, and some organizational. We all consist of a bundle of diversities.[4] That is "intersectionality." People of color often find race to be the most salient of those myriad dimensions.

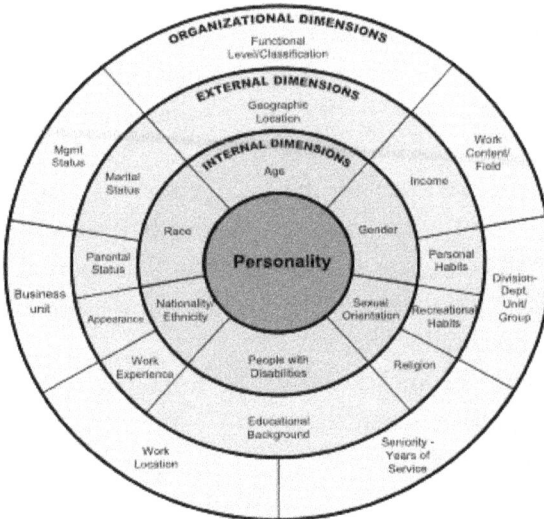

## Cultural Competence

Central to engaging with DEI is cultural competence, which speaks to operationalizing DEI through skill-building. Cultural competence recognizes that every entity develops a culture, and, ideally, that culture reflects an openness to and respect for all, within and without.

Organizational culture consists of its formal and informal policies, procedures, programs, and processes, and incorporates certain values, beliefs, assumptions, and customs. To be culturally competent, an entity develops peoples' awareness, attitudes, knowledge, and skills around DEI, and works to transform its culture through standards, policies, and practices that affirm all.

Schools offer a vivid example:

> Social justice is about distributing resources fairly and treating all students equitably so that they feel safe and secure—physically and psychologically.... Bringing social justice into schools shines a spotlight on all sorts of important societal issues—from the myriad reasons that lie beneath the deep disparity between the suspension rates of black and white students to how current U.S. immigration policy separates families and violates student rights.[5]

The need for culturally competent educators skilled at addressing the many needs of an increasingly diverse student population is both evident and urgent. Contextually, cultural competence in school settings requires, at a minimum, attention to:

- *Delivery (e.g.,* creating awareness of and tailoring to different learning styles; managing power dynamics so as to engage all learners);
- *Content (e.g.,* presenting complete, accurate content; considering multiple perspectives);
- *Teaching and learning materials (e.g.,* ensuring that materials are substantive, varied, and as objective as possible);
- *Perspective (e.g.,* presenting content through a variety of lenses rather than offering a singular view);
- *Inclusivity (e.g.,* engaging students at multiple levels; facilitating student learning with and from their fellow students);

- *Civic and social responsibility* (*e.g.*, paying attention to social justice issues; contemplating what makes for a good citizen in our American democracy); and
- *Assessment* (*e.g.*, evaluating the curriculum for substantive accuracy and bias).[6]

Calls for enhanced cultural competence in public school leadership grow louder. Educational leadership programs face ongoing demands to ramp up curricula around DEI and social justice issues.

> Principals . . . must confront a number of unique challenges when working with a student population where the majority of students are considered to be at-risk for school failure, and thus the principals must have the capacity to engage in, and facilitate, social justice-oriented conversations with students, parents, and community stakeholders. Consequently, leadership preparation programs [should] purposefully address issues of diversity and social justice, ensuring these matters are woven throughout the written curricula upon which these programs are founded [citations omitted].[7]

## The Case for DEI

When we engage people around DEI, we ground them in the structural, institutional, and systemic bases of the social justice issues that need to be addressed.

In the 21st century, to ignore DEI—to take the status quo route—is to be content with mediocrity. That is because achieving excellence demands we cast a wider net, tap into the full potential of everyone, and allow all individuals to become and be their best selves.

When a community (*i.e.*, educational, residential, cultural, commercial, recreational, or other entity or space) is perceived as welcoming, nurturing, and supporting by and for all, it attracts the best and the brightest and, as a result, it achieves at higher levels.

People seek places where they can learn and grow; where they are met with both clear expectations and the resources needed to meet them; and where fairness, trust, and respect are core values.

When we fully embrace DEI, we will be able to leverage synergies from the people, creativity, and connections we have encouraged, supported, and nurtured.

Dr. Martin Luther King, Jr. captured a profound truth when he noted that "we will come together as brothers and sisters or we will perish together as fools." Dr. King also said we are "caught in an inescapable network of mutuality; tied in a single garment of destiny.... I can never be what I ought to be until you are what you ought to be. You can never be what you ought to be until I am what I ought to be." We are better together.

Exceptional leaders recognize the connections and shared fate that unite us all. They build on that commonality of interest in ways that bring us together and embolden us to confront the challenges we face head-on.

We build community when we communicate effectively across the various dimensions of diversity, support one another, and collaborate around our shared values and toward common goals.

We build community when we view DEI not as a problem to be solved, but rather as a reality to be acknowledged, understood, and embraced.

We build community when we change not just individual mindsets, but systems and institutions, too.

The absence of an appreciation of DEI may result in a range of behaviors, from exclusive and demeaning words and rhetoric to genocide. Ignorance enhances exposure.

Two rationales support the case for DEI: one moral, the

other economic (*i.e.*, business). It is, simply put, both right and smart.

The moral case for DEI is straightforward. Treating others with respect and affirming the humanity of every person—those are universal values grounded in most national, cultural, and religious traditions. It is the right thing to do.

The economic case is equally clear. When businesses embrace DEI, they experience heightened competitive advantage in a global economy; broadened creativity and innovation; expanded perspectives; improved products and services; reduced turnover (and hence, lower training costs); enlarged markets; lowered health care costs (as a result of a more supportive, nurturing workplace); enhanced employee self-image; decreased risk of employment litigation; and elevated community profile and standing. A DEI investment today yields dividends well into the future.[8]

The diversity dividend, the return on inclusion, is more than worth the investment of time, talent, and treasure we put into crafting environments that are welcoming and nurturing for all. Yes, we are different from one another, often in significant ways, but what we have in common—our shared humanity—overarches our differences.

Embracing DEI is not about masking our differences. It is not about using our differences as wedges, either. Rather, it is about celebrating our differences while being mindful of our shared humanity.

From the richness of DEI, we: build individual and collective self-awareness and self-esteem; draw the motivation and inspiration essential to innovation; gain insight and perspective otherwise lacking in decision-making; and expand the depth and breadth of our reach into communities. That is just part of what we reap when we sow the seeds of DEI.

DEI can be a catalyst for progress, but likely not without tension. Working through that tension, however, is worth the periodic discomfort we may feel as we encounter, size up, and accept the different and the unknown.

## DEI Moments

By listening to others as they narrate their firsthand experiences, we can better understand and appreciate DEI. I call these stories "DEI Moments."

Most of us can recall at least one significant incident that reminded us we were somehow "different," whether because of gender, race, ethnicity, national origin, religion, ability status, sexual orientation, gender identify, age, economic status, or some other dimensions of diversity. Such incidents typically involve exercises of power and privilege by some "other" at our expense.

DEI Moments may be events we experienced directly or occurrences we witnessed. Though often negative and sometimes referred to as "micro-aggressions," DEI Moments may be positive, too.

DEI Moments—instances forever seared into our memory —are part of the baggage so many of us carry. Take time to reflect on one of your DEI Moments.

DEI Moments shared with me in workshops and other settings gave me pause. I think of them often.

I remember the Black man who said, "In high school, I told my principal that I wanted to go to college. My principal said: 'You'll be in state prison by the time you're twenty-one.'"

I recall the white man who reflected, "I'm white. I thought of myself as a tolerant person. I was recently watching a television show with my eleven-year-old son. The show featured a Black family. I told my son, 'Isn't it amazing how articulate this Black family is?' My son replied, 'Yes, Dad, but isn't it amazing that you are amazed?'"

I think of the Black woman who said, "A white lady saw

my little girl and asked to pick her up. Then she said, 'She's one of the cleanest ones I've seen in a long time.'"

I remember the woman who declared, "My son's seventh-grade basketball team was scheduled to play in their league's semifinal game on a Saturday morning. As luck would have it, there was also a Bar Mitzvah that morning and the whole team had been invited. The boys themselves voted to request that the game time be changed. The league refused to honor the request. The boys then all agreed to forfeit the game and attend the Bar Mitzvah."

Another woman recounted, "My husband's brother died of AIDS. He was gay and because of family and religious pressure, he did not stay in a monogamous relationship. A week after his death and funeral, my husband and I were with our closest friends when they started to tell AIDS jokes. My husband was not able to tell them his brother was gay and had died of AIDS. I had to respect his wishes and remain quiet while our friends said things that hurt us both deeply."

Yet another woman recalled, "I went to work one day and requested a raise, only to be told by my boss, 'You are married. Your husband makes lots of money.'"

And then there was the young man who offered, "I suffered an injury at age eighteen that left me paralyzed from the waist down and wheelchair-bound. At one point following my injury, I went to an ice cream shop with my grandmother. The shop attendant looked at me, and then asked my grand-mother, 'What does *he* want?'"

There was also a woman who said, "I went shopping with my wheel-chair-bound child. An older, well-dressed woman came up to me and asked, 'How can you bring such a poor little thing out in public?'"

Finally, there was the woman who shared, "I moved to a new town and began visiting churches, looking for a home church. At one stop, a lady asked, 'Where's your husband?' I replied that I was divorced and raising my children alone. She then said, 'Well, you're a divorcee. You won't be welcome here because the married women won't be comfortable with you being around their husbands. Perhaps you should find another church.'"

These DEI Moments are rooted in the same phenomena as the broader social justice ills and inequities that plague us (*e.g.*, racism, sexism, homophobia, and classism; otherization and dehumanization). They remind us we can do better; we should do better; we must *be* better.

## Exploring Our DEI Baggage

One simple activity designed to explore our DEI baggage is "Different and the Same," which examines the realities of race/ethnicity/color vis-à-vis power and privilege. The exercise asks people to "walk a mile in someone else's shoes"—someone from a different racial, ethnic, or cultural background.

Imagine you woke up tomorrow morning and discovered that you belonged to another racial, ethnic, or cultural group. Ask yourself which aspects of your life would be different, and which would be the same?

This simple exercise recalls the real-world experiment created by journalist John Howard Griffin and chronicled in the 1961 book, *Black Like Me.*[9] Griffin, a white man, discovered the slights, indignities, and humiliations borne of race by altering his appearance and "passing" as a Black man in the Deep South.

A firm grounding in DEI gives us insight into the social, political, and economic history and present-day realities that provide the backdrop for social justice issues. It also nurtures the impulse to empathy that is essential in addressing such issues.

---
FRAMING SOCIAL JUSTICE
---

"We will all profit from a more diverse, inclusive society, understanding, accommodating, even celebrating our differences, while pulling together for the common good."[10]

— JUSTICE RUTH BADER GINSBERG

## POINTS TO PONDER

What baggage do you carry (or have you carried) around DEI and how will you deal with it (or how have you dealt with it)?

What were the advantages and disadvantages of your upbringing vis-à-vis others (*e.g.*, financial, educational, familial) and how have you dealt with them?

How inclusive is your circle and, if it is not as inclusive as you would like, how will you work to expand it?

Suppose you have been asked to create a personal mantra—a slogan—about DEI. What would be your words of wisdom?

## 5

# 10 WAYS WE CAN ADVANCE SOCIAL JUSTICE

"Freedom is incomplete without social justice."[1]

— ATAL BIHARI VAJPAYEE

WHEN IT COMES TO ADVANCING SOCIAL JUSTICE, WE MUST know, care, *and act*. Our all-too-ready default, offering our "thoughts and prayers" ("TAPS"), is evidence of knowing and caring. It conveys the required seriousness associated with injustice of any sort. But while rendering TAPS may be necessary, it is woefully insufficient to meet the moment. *Action* must be added to the mix.

Contemplate how the average person with a heart for social justice might translate that passion into action. Consider the following 10 Ways We Can Advance Social Justice.

1. **Speak truth.**
2. **Listen intently.**
3. **Show up.**
4. **Engage with your community.**
5. **Seek to serve.**
6. **Align with allies.**

7. **Play politics.**
8. **Delve into Diversity, Equity & Inclusion.**
9. **Pledge allegiance.**
10. **Walk the walk.**[2]

**1. Speak truth:** Spread empowering information, whether through word of mouth to friends and family, via social media and e-mails, or just by having a conversation with colleagues at work. Call out misinformation and disinformation, which threaten to poison the well of democracy.

Truth travels fast but lies travel faster. If people do not know about social justice issues, they cannot care, and if they do not care, they will not act. People must *know*, *care*, and *act* if social justice is to prevail.

Speak *your truth*—what you think, what you believe, what you experienced, what you feel—after you have done your research; educate yourself. Understand that others may have differing perspectives. Be open to new and contradicting information and the possibility, however remote, that data may dictate a change of course.

The *way* one speaks truth matters. Making demands tends to shut down the target. The word "demand" means "an insistent and peremptory request, made as if by right."[3] Implicitly, demands tend cast the target as malevolent and blame-worthy. People who feel put upon are more likely to be combative than cooperative or collaborative.

Speak truth in ways that allow others to hear it, embrace it as their own, and act upon the message. That requires maturity.

Speaking truth and the next step, listening intently, are essential to the dialogue needed to make progress on social justice issues.

Dialogue deepens and widens bilateral understanding and allows us to learn about ourselves and the people with whom we are engaged. People share their views, attitudes, beliefs, and feelings about a subject.[4]

EXAMPLE: Anytown, Oklahoma, the summer youth leadership and diversity experience referenced earlier, works because the teens speak their truth. The camp allows them the time and space to be who they are or who they are becoming without judgment. They present authentically and are received in the same vein.

Honesty, genuineness, and authenticity must be facilitated and cultivated. At Anytown, establishing ground rules at the outset and letting teens know, "You may not always feel comfortable, but you should always feel safe," sets the stage. Trained staff reinforce these messages throughout the experience.

Anytown is admittedly a bubble—an idealized setting unlikely to be replicated in the real world. That said, it simulates what the real-world possibilities could be while allowing teens to soul-search—to find and reveal themselves in the context of a supportive community.

Speaking truth has both external and internal dimensions. We should speak truth to and about others, but, perhaps more importantly, we should speak truth to and about ourselves.

**Accentuating Adage:** "The way to right wrongs is to shine the light of truth upon them."[5]

— IDA B. WELLS-BARNETT

**2. Listen intently:** Be courteous and open to hearing what others think and feel. Listening can be an illuminating and validating process for all. Listening to alternative perspectives, even those with which we vehemently disagree, is a prerequisite to dialogue and an essential ingredient in the recipe for understanding.[6]

Listen actively—listen to understand. Empathic listening helps build strong relationships, promotes a fuller understanding of others, and deepens the listener's own sense of empathy.[7]

Listen affirmatively—with an open mind and with a view toward better grasping the other's perspective—instead of negatively—with a view toward fashioning a response. Listening does not imply acceptance.

It takes equal measures of humility and discipline to listen intently, particularly when one hears challenging, contrary, and non-confirming information. To lend a listening ear—to truly listen—is to extend grace; to offer another a too-often-rare opportunity to share in a non-judgmental, safe context. It may be a challenge for all concerned, but the probable payoff —shared understanding and potential progress—is well worth any temporary discomfort.

EXAMPLE: In the late 1990s, I served on the Board of Directors (and later as Board President) of Leadership Tulsa, one of the nation's first community leadership organizations. Founded in 1973, Leadership Tulsa identifies and develops leaders who catalyze community change and who are in many instances champions of social justice.

Leadership Tulsa does not have a social justice mission *per se*. Rather, the group explicitly brings together people across lines of difference—people who often become the agents of change that social justice demands.

For the first two-decades-plus of its history, Leadership Tulsa refrained from taking public stances on community issues, largely out of concern for the perils of political partisanship and the risk of endangering its tax-favored Section 501(c)(3) status with the Internal Revenue Service.

Former Tulsa Public Schools Superintendent John Thompson, in office from 1994 to 2000, served on the Leadership Tulsa board of directors from 1994 to 1997. I served as President-Elect during the 1996 – 1997 fiscal year.[8]

During his Leadership Tulsa board tenure, Dr. Thompson lobbied the organization for its public support of a 1996 school district bond issue to fund significant system-wide improvements. In Oklahoma, school district bond issues must be approved by a 60% supermajority of voters. At the time, such bond issues had become less popular, so achieving the supermajority needed for passage was in no way guaranteed.

Dr. Thompson questioned Leadership Tulsa's unwritten policy against taking public stances on community issues. He wanted board members, who had significant community networks and could, in his estimation, bring out the "yes" votes, to officially support the bond issue—to be ambassadors for the cause.

Board members listened—cautiously, skeptically—but they listened. They almost universally supported the bond issue in principle. However, they expressed concerns about setting a precedent—about endorsing the bond issue and then being besieged with requests for Leadership Tulsa to endorse this cause or that.

The board kept an open mind, listened, and was willing to rethink its absolute ban on taking stances on public issues. Dr. Thompson's argument about the dire need for school improvements gained traction and ultimately won them over.

Speaking with media at the time, Tamara Rains, Leadership Tulsa Board President, emphasized the groundbreaking nature of the bond issue endorsement: "Leadership Tulsa's endorsement is a marked departure from the past. Up until this point, Leadership Tulsa had never publicly endorsed a community issue or initiative. Leadership Tulsa's endorsement speaks volumes about the significance of education to the overall well-being of our shared community."[9]

Ultimately, Tulsa voters approved two bond issues during Dr. Thompson's tenure, one for about $94.5 million in 1996 and another for $109 million in 1999.[10]

As a result of the bond controversy, Leadership Tulsa

adopted a specific policy delineating criteria that must be met prior to taking a public stance on a community issue. Most notably, any such action must be consistent with the mission work of Leadership Tulsa.

The original iteration of the community issues policy required a 60% supermajority vote of the board of directors to approve taking such a public stance. An updated policy affirmed and bolstered the supermajority requirement. Now, a *unanimous* vote of the Leadership Tulsa board of directors must undergird any public stance on a community issue.[11]

Edward H. Richards got it right in his poem, "The Owl."

"A wise old owl sat on an oak,
The more he saw the
less he spoke;
The less he spoke the more
he heard;
Why aren't we like that
wise old bird?"

**Accentuating Adage:** "To just know a truth is not enough. First, you must understand. And it requires bravery from two people. One to speak it. And one to listen."[12]

— ANA JOHNS

**3. Show up:** Showing up implies more than mere physical presence. To really show up, one has to be mentally focused and emotionally centered.

Situate yourself among people of purpose and passion. Attending community meetings, rallies, protests, peaceful demonstrations, or other group events offers: an opening to engage with similarly enthusiastic people in ways that nurture and sustain the drive to be a change-maker; an occasion to express individual and group views on political (and other) issues; a way to relieve tension/frustration as a sort of release valve or catharsis; a vehicle by which to promote or champion a cause or position; a chance to catalyze change; a way to expand the circle—be part of something larger than oneself; and an opportunity for an infusion of inspiration from those who join you in the cause.

Ongoing motivation is especially important in social justice work, where challenges are often colossal, and change is most often incremental. Even choir members need to receive the word to be reinforced and rejuvenated around their passion points. Sometimes a critical mass of passion, commitment, and focus provides the energy that allows us to go the extra mile.

The maxim, "Get in where you fit in," applies. We should each engage with the social justice issue(s) around which our passion lies. We should enter at the point and level that best suits us.

EXAMPLE: It is all too easy to say "yes." By answering in the affirmative, we avoid (at least temporarily) uncomfortable conversations and potential conflict, we satisfy our own ego (we can, in fact, "do it all"), and we accumulate more tokens for the resume.

Sometimes, it is just "niceness" that compels a "yes" response. I am guilty of occasionally having said yes to things out of courtesy instead of passion. The temporary comfort of pleasing others (often, the person who extended an invitation) soon gives way to the discomfort of inactivity and inaction; of time misspent and energy misplaced.

As a professional Black male in a predominantly white community—and an overwhelmingly white *professional* community—I frequently get asked to serve on nonprofit boards. Early on, I routinely accepted such invitations, in part out of politeness and in part borne of a desire to have people like me reflected and/or represented among the governance ranks of community organizations.

I soon discovered my good intentions needed to match my passion in order for things to work out. That is, for me to really "show up," I needed to have a commitment deeper than to courtesy and representation. I need to have a commitment to the mission of the organization I was being asked to serve and excitement about helping further that mission.

I learned to decline, politely, invitations that did not ignite a fire within, and to suggest other individuals who both might reflect diversity and be committed to the cause. In so doing, I reserved time for those things around which my passion lies.

Showing up is important, and that means being both physically and mentally present. Sometimes, "just say no" is good advice. Saying "yes" comes with a commitment to show up that may be beyond our level of interest and readiness.

**Accentuating Adage:** "Decisions are made by those who show up."[13]

— AARON SORKIN

**4. Engage with your community:** The term "community" embodies this sense of service and sacrifice, suggesting our fundamental connectedness. Taking an interest in the interests of others therefore becomes a matter of self-interest. Community service teaches, by precept and by example, the undeniably exhilarating and empowering concept of the human family—of mutual relationships, mutual respect, and mutual responsibility.

Community service is also an investment in social capital —in building sustainable relationships grounded in mutual trust and reciprocal responsibility that lift all, not just those who are actively engaged.

Social capital, the value of social networks that bond similar people and bridge between diverse people, leverages individual capacities for group gains. Simply stated, it is the goodwill we leverage from our positive relationships with others, whether through sharing information and resources, providing aid and assistance, or relying upon trust built over time through meaningful, positive interactions.

Often overlooked and undervalued, social capital is among the ties that bind. Though not readily quantified and monetized, it brings inestimable value to individuals and communities. Arguably, racial reconciliation is one of many potential returns on an investment in social capital in general, and trust-building in particular.

In Tulsa, I have since 2008 facilitated the Mayor's Police and Community Coalition ("MPACC"). The group emerged from community conversations about the need for citizen oversight of the police and builds the bonds of trust between the Tulsa Police Department and the diverse constituent communities it serves. Members include the Mayor, Police Chief, TPD officers, and representatives from various racial, ethnic, cultural, religious, and other communities.

MPACC connects people. It seeds relationships, and then harvests social capital. This loosely-knit, largely informal group meets bi-monthly for topical presentations and updates from the Chief of Police. We participate in police ride-alongs, host public forums, and sponsor an annual youth summit for high school students, the centerpiece of which is our "tabletop cops" segment—an opportunity for youth to get up close and personal with police officers and ask whatever questions that come to mind.

How does MPACC leverage the one-on-one relationships it builds? How does it trade in social capital? One example stands out.

EXAMPLE: In the early morning hours of Sunday, June 12, 2016, forty-nine people were killed and fifty-three wounded in a mass shooting at Pulse, a gay nightclub in Orlando, Florida. Orlando police officers shot and killed the assailant after a three-hour standoff. It remains the deadliest incident in the history of violence against the LGBTQ community in the United States.[14]

Chuck Jordan, then TPD Chief, learned of the incident and immediately contacted Toby Jenkins, then CEO/Executive Director of the Equality Center in Tulsa, one of the largest LGBTQ centers in the region. Chief Jordan knew Jenkins through their mutual affiliation with MPACC.

The Chief informed a stunned Jenkins of the tragedy, then asked if there was anything TPD needed to do to protect the needs of the LGBTQ community in Tulsa.

Jenkins will not soon forget that call:

> Chief Jordan called me at 8:00 a.m. on Sunday morning as I was getting ready for church. I had no idea what he was talking about. He was the first person to tell me. Within twenty minutes, I arrived at the Equality Center, which had nine police cars surrounding it. Later that evening, a community vigil took place at Club Majestic [a gay nightclub] and ended in a candlelight vigil at Guthrie Green [a public park]. TPD surrounded us with heads bowed, as over 1,000 LGBTQ community members provided us with safety to grieve. The Tulsa skyline was lit with skyscrapers that had turned their towers rainbow. In that first twenty-four hours, no one knew if it was a strategic terrorist plot with other targets yet to come. That same day, there had been several other suspicious incidents across the country. Chief Jordan wanted a list of the gay bars, LGBTQ spaces, and other possible targets.[15]

Chief Jordan's display of compassion and empathy speaks to the value of relationship-building; of laying the foundation upon which trust is built.

Jordan and Jenkins had spoken a number of times via MPACC. They had one another's cell phone number. They felt a mutual connection around community safety and security. This moment solidified that.

The interaction between Jordan and Jenkins also illustrates leadership. Community and social justice require that we see beyond ourselves and understand our connectedness to others.

All of us have a moral obligation to return to the community at least some small portion of that which we have been given; a moral obligation to lead—to share our individual gifts with others so as to inspire, guide, and facilitate the achievement of worthwhile goals.

Ultimately, many have found that the search for meaning in life ends with the discovery of altruism—with living lives in such a way as to positively impact the lives of others. There is no better feeling, no better character enhancer, than the satisfaction and fulfillment of serving others—putting someone else before oneself.

America is a society of diverse elements with disparate interests borne of history, culture, and tradition. Yet, what we share in common far outweighs our differences. Our various societal groupings—racial, ethnic, religious, cultural, just to name a few—cannot and do not exist as islands wholly separate from our common and shared culture. Ultimately, we are interdependent. Both as individuals and as distinct racial, ethnic, religious, and cultural groups, we cannot possibly reach our full human potential without some level of interaction with other individuals and other groups, without embracing altruism.

Why focus so much on what divides us? Why not direct our gaze toward that which connects us—what we share in common? We can find ways to build bridges which span the vast gulfs of division and difference.

Get to know your neighbors. Together, mobilize for change. Start a community dialogue. One cannot promote social justice on a broader level without engaging first at a community level.

Community dialogue, particularly around race, can create a powerful dynamic conducive to positive change.

> A [community] dialogue is a forum that draws participants from as many parts of the community as possible to exchange information face-to-face, share personal stories and experiences, honestly express perspectives, clarify viewpoints, and develop solutions to community concerns.
>
> Unlike debate, dialogue emphasizes listening to deepen understanding…. Dialogue invites discovery. It develops common values and allows participants to express their own interests. It expects that participants will grow in understanding and may decide to act together with common goals. In dialogue, participants can question and reevaluate their assumptions. Through this process, people are learning to work together to improve race relations.[16]

Grassroots movements—organic efforts—can be both strong and sustainable and can provide the inspiration for larger initiatives. Being good stewards of the various communities to which we belong, is critical. Community stewardship —the careful and responsible management of the community entrusted to our care—implies vision, trust, accountability, responsibility, strategic planning, fiscal and financial integrity, and fairness.

When engaging with community, the simple things matter. If we seek to build and maintain positive, affirming relationships, both personally and professionally, then we should keep some basic precepts like authenticity, honesty, and grace in mind.

When it comes to engaging with your community to advance social justice, know your role—being able to get in where you fit in—is paramount. We all have a role to play, but we do not all have the same role to play.

Bill Moyers, in *The Four Roles of Social Activism*, identified critical roles that, taken together, propel change: citizen; reformer; rebel; and change agent.[17]

The *citizen* is seen as engaged and responsible and enjoys the respect and trust of the majority of ordinary people. The *reformer* operates, structurally, from within and works with the official political and judicial structures to integrate solutions into laws, policies, and practices, both public and private. The *rebel* calls out hypocrisy and inequity in direct and public ways. The *change agent* educates, organizes, and mobilizes the general public in support of social justice ends.

We may have a bit of each of these in us, but more than likely we tend toward one or two of these roles as we take on social justice activism. My "zone" straddles the roles of *citizen* and *change agent.*

EXAMPLE: My late parents, Frank and Bernice West Johnson, instilled in me a love of education and a commitment to community service. They modeled grit and gumption, their legacy gifts from the Carter and West families rooted in rural Arkansas.

My father, a World War II veteran, educator, and employment counselor, led and served publicly, primarily through the NAACP. My mother, always a country girl at heart, led quietly and privately, mainly through her church work.

In the realm of community service, it was the up-close-and-personal examples I saw that influenced and molded me —the exemplary lives lived by these modest, humble individuals who did the best they could with what they had.

Both vocally and actively supported my education, showing up for PTA meetings, student council functions, band concerts, pancake breakfasts, spaghetti suppers, graduations, and everything in between. When it came to education, their support was unconditional and unwavering.

I am who I am because they were who they were. They are gone, but never forgotten. They are with me in spirit.

One of my Mother's treasured adages was: "Give me my flowers while I yet live." I tried to do just that—to let both my parents know, through word and deed, how much they meant to me. My community engagement, my work to advance social justice, is a bouquet, both for them and for me.

**Accentuating Adage:** "The greatness of a community is most accurately measured by the compassionate actions of its members."[18]

— CORETTA SCOTT KING

**5. Seek to serve:** Find opportunities to help those in need, including organizations and initiatives whose core work supports those who are often forgotten or marginalized. There are programs that address the social justice issues that appeal to you. Seek them out. Find out where you fit in.

Volunteer. Make a financial contribution. Consider service on the organization's governance board when you are ready (*i.e.*, governance board service requires appropriate knowledge and training, and generally entails reciprocal commitments and obligations between the board member and the organization served).

Inventory and leverage your birthright gifts—strength, compassion, and courage, among others—in service to the larger community and social justice.[19]

EXAMPLE: I am drawn to social justice organizations and programs that support education and prepare young people for community service. Anytown is one obvious example. Leadership Tulsa is another. My work with Tulsa's now-defunct Urban League is yet another.

The challenges I confront most often (*e.g.*, racism and

other DEI issues) are chronic. I see part of my role as helping identify, develop, and support a corps of individuals who will conduct this work beyond me. Stated differently, I see a key part of my role as empowering other people, especially those who look like me (*i.e.*, people of color), by facilitating their development and connecting them with individuals and groups who have access to the centers of power and privilege that can propel them forward.

Two prominent nonprofits in Tulsa, Leadership Tulsa and the Tulsa Area United Way, initiated a program called "New Voices" in 2009.[20] I participated in the discussions that led to the creation of the program and crafted curricular materials, mostly focused on nonprofit governance and management, for the program retreat.

Nonprofits called out for a lack of diverse leadership often point to the lack of a pool of candidates of color from which to draw board members. New Voices set out to increase diversity on nonprofit boards in the Tulsa area by developing a reservoir of talent among individuals from historically underrepresented racial, cultural, ethnic, and religious groups.

Part of my service obligation is to the future. I see an aspect of my social justice role as that of seed sower.

**Accentuating Adage:** "The best way to find yourself is to lose yourself in the service of others."[21]

— MAHATMA GANDHI

**6. Align with allies:** Seek and stand in solidarity with groups who regularly fight for equality, equity, and the basic human rights for all. As has been so often said, "Injustice anywhere is a threat to justice everywhere."[22] Support, financially and otherwise, the organizations whose mission work centers on eliminating disparities based on the dimensions of diversity.

Alignment often starts online. Consider a couple of the more prominent social justice movements of the recent past: #blacklivesmatter (focusing, as previously noted, on the killing of unarmed young Black men—and some women—by police and improving Black community relations with law enforcement) and #metoo (focused, primarily, on sexual harassment and sexual assault by men on women, most often in situations where there is a power imbalance). These online movements generate buzz and expand the reach of and support for the social justice issues to which they are dedicated.

Social media affords global access to organizations that enhance visibility and expand networking. Skillfully employed, social media amplifies voices, supercharges information dissemination, and fosters collaboration.

That said, discernment is in order. As much as it can be a vehicle for good, so, too, can social media be an instrument for evil. Most of us are aware of instances in which social media spread untruths, fomented hatred, or instigated violence.

For motivation and inspiration about the power of allies, consider the prospect of a world in which these social justice organizations did not exist—a world without the NAACP, the NAACP Legal Defense Fund, the Equal Justice Initiative, the Anti-Defamation League, the Southern Poverty Law Center, La Raza, the National Urban League, the National Organization for Women, the Human Rights Campaign, the Children's Defense Fund, 100 Black Men of America, Inc., the Council on American-Islamic Relations, and so many more.[23] A world absent these trailblazing organizations would be a world in which I cannot imagine living.

EXAMPLE: Too often we seek to do what is already being done, in part out of ignorance, but sometimes on account of ego. We fail to take the time to see who out there is doing the work that needs to be done—and doing it well. Cooperation and collaboration may be better options than competition. In Tulsa, leading philanthropists incentivize and sometimes forge collaboration. The operative question is: "Who is best suited to do this work?" Ideally, those with a heart for the work and the finances to support it will find their way to those best equipped to implement it.

I try to support the people and organizations doing the kinds of social justice work I value most with at least one of the three Ts: time, talent, and treasure. My support, active or passive, matters.

I am humble enough to know I need not always do the work myself. If another person or organization does it better, more power to them.

Coalitions bring organizations together around a common purpose or mission. This form of allyship lends structure and focus to shared social justice ends.

A longstanding Tulsa-based group, the "Say No To Hate Coalition," is illustrative. Established in 1988 in response to a growing white supremacist skinhead movement, the Coalition is an open-ended volunteer network of community-based and civic organizations.[24]

Community leaders and advocates established the Coalition as a forum in which to share information, trends, and best practices in the area of DEI generally. More specifically, the Coalition monitors and addresses hate-based activity in the Tulsa area and builds bridges, through networking and dialogue, which help connect all sectors of Tulsa.

Early on, the Coalition's first-order objectives included: eliminating hate-based bigotry and violence; inclusivity in all community planning and strategic processes; increasing understanding of the identities and experiences of all members of the community through curricular and other educational initiatives; and providing positive DEI leadership.

Tulsa civic leader Yolanda Charney founded the group.

Working with the Jewish Federation of Tulsa in 1988, Charney and others in the Jewish community noticed an uptick in anti-Semitic graffiti and vandalism. The timing coincided with the 50th anniversary of Kristallnacht, the night of widespread looting of Jewish businesses and synagogues in Germany in 1938, generally considered the dawn of some of the darkest days in our history, the Holocaust.

In the fall of 1988, White Aryan Resistance founder Tom Metzger targeted Tulsa for a recruiting drive. The then-prominent white supremacist personally visited Tulsa.

Jewish community leaders met with Black community leaders, Tulsa city officials, and human rights organizations. Charney and Rev. Lawrence Lakey, then executive director of the Metropolitan Urban League, crafted a press release. They alerted the media to their joint statement extolling Tulsa's achievements and ongoing work in the realm of interfaith, intercultural, and human relations (*i.e.*, what would now fall under the DEI umbrella) and declaring Metzger's group unwelcome in the city. Metzger, feeling the lack of love, cut short his visit.

Despite this early win, the white supremacist skinhead movement crossed the line from ideology to violence in places across the country. Incidents in Tulsa and Oklahoma City spurred the creation of a statewide response campaign and coalition. The Oklahoma Attorney General at the time, Robert Henry, agreed to be the Honorary Chair of the statewide body. Tulsa leadership reached out to Oklahoma City leaders Leonard Benton, Rabbi David Packman, and Mark Schwartz for additional, statewide support.

Religious, educational, law enforcement, and human relations communities coalesced and organized a statewide conference on organized hate. These groups convened at the State Capitol on November 9 – 10, 1988, the 50th anniversary of Kristallnacht. The event featured prominent speakers from Oklahoma and beyond.[25]

I participated in the Coalition from the outset through my involvement with OCCJ. While I recall countless meaningful and memorable moments, none stands out like the "Silent Sweep Against Hate" on October 1, 2000.

The Ku Klux Klan scheduled a rally in downtown Tulsa on Saturday, September 30, 2000. That date coincided with Rosh Hashanah, the Jewish New Year. The Coalition decided to send a message of inclusion and tolerance to the Tulsa community by discouraging attendance at a counter-demonstration coincident with the KKK rally. The thinking was that a counter-demonstration would only enhance the visibility of the KKK, playing directly into its hands.

In lieu of staging a counter-demonstration or supporting one, the Coalition encouraged its members to come with family, friends, neighbors, and co-workers to a "Silent Sweep Against Hate" on Sunday, October 1, 2000, the day following the KKK rally.

Many participants donned OCCJ-provided tee shirts that proclaimed, in boldface lettering: "**JOIN OUR HATE GROUP. We hate racism. We hate prejudice. We hate bigotry.**" The provocative and mildly controversial shirts were originally designed for a multi-media public awareness campaign.

Coalition members brought brooms, mops, buckets and trash bags for a cleaning of the site of the previous day's KKK rally. No agenda. No program. No speeches. The Silent Sweep Against Hate simply and symbolically removed any taint of exclusion and bigotry left by the KKK rally.

This pointed, powerful, and profound social justice event furthered the mission work of the Coalition, cemented relationships among allies, and raised the Coalition's community profile.

**Accentuating Adage:** "There is only one thing worse than fighting with allies, and that is fighting without them."[26]

— WINSTON CHURCHILL

**7. Play politics:** The First Amendment to the United States Constitution recognizes five rights, the last of which is the right to petition the government for the redress of grievances. The right to petition links social (and individual) responsibility with governmental accountability.

Literary legend James Baldwin once said: "It is inconceivable that a sovereign people continue, as we do so abjectly, to say, 'I can't do anything about it. It's the government.' The government is the creation of the people. It is responsible to the people. And the people are responsible for it."[27]

Key structures, institutions, and systems are influenced, if not controlled, by governmental (*i.e.*, political) actors, and they need to be changed if disparities and inequities are to be diminished or, ideally, eliminated. We are the agents of change.

Stay informed about issues by attending school board and civic meetings, reviewing relevant politicians' websites, tracking proposed legislation, and subscribing to newsletters, bulletins, and alerts.

Correspond with your elected representatives about the social justice issues that matter to you. Share your views and advice in e-mails, phone calls, or by other means.

Most politicians respond to constituent feedback, and many get less direct contact from citizens than one might imagine. Sending a text or an e-mail, making a phone call, or writing an old-school letter are simple ways to let your representatives know where you stand.

Remember, politicians shape the landscape for social justice by virtue of the legislative and legal framework they create or forestall. Let them hear from you about your priorities and passions. They work for you, and presumably you are a voter. (If you are not, you should be.) They have something to lose if they choose to ignore or dismiss you.

Vote. Work on a political campaign. Seek elective office if you are so inclined. Lead change.

Politically, our world is on fire. In what feels like the blink of an eye, the slow burn of politics morphed into a raging wildfire. Our votes are the flame retardants at our disposal to tamp down the inferno.

The words of President Abraham Lincoln resonate: "Elections belong to the people. It's their decision. If they decide to turn their back on the fire and burn their behinds, then they will just have to sit on their blisters." We decide whether crass partisanship, corrosive divisiveness, and unchecked incivility dominate or whether, ultimately, democracy reigns.

Think of politics broadly, extending beyond legislative, executive, and judicial office holders. Bodies closer to the community level like school boards and parent-teacher associations, though ideally not partisan, are indeed political. Think about all the ways we can plug in politically: registering voters, working the polls, boning up on history and civics, supporting a cause, attending town hall meetings, and showing up at city council meetings.[28] Your views and your voice matter.

Understand that in politics, as in life, failure is inevitable—unavoidable—but seldom permanent. Among famous failures are some of our most celebrated icons: Thomas Edison, Walt Disney, Albert Einstein, Bill Gates, and Oprah Winfrey.

Thomas Edison failed more than 10,000 times while attempting to create a commercially viable light bulb. Walt Disney's first company went bankrupt. Einstein, mute until age four, failed a secondary school entrance exam and at his first job. Bill Gates' first software company failed. Oprah Winfrey was fired from her first television job.

They failed, but not permanently. They did not become failures. Their disappointments fueled their destinies.[29]

Allow failure to be a lesson in humility. Leverage it for future success. With each experience, ask: "What is this meant to teach me?" As Dr. King so eloquently noted, "We must accept finite disappointments, but we must never lose infinite hope."

EXAMPLE: Just keeping abreast of the myriad issues at play can be a challenge. It is necessary, though, if we are to move closer to social justice. Key issues are most often structural, systemic, and institutional. Much of the potentially meaningful change lies in the hands of politicians.

My parents, Bernice and Frank Johnson, instilled in me the imperative of playing politics—of political participation. They did so by their powerful example. Both born in Arkansas in the early 1920s, they understood what it meant not to be able to vote, whether by law or in fact.

They played politics. They voted. *They always voted.*

Vote. Vote for school board members. Vote for city councilors and mayors. Vote for county and state officials. Vote for congressional representatives. Vote for President of these United States.

Vote. Vote on local ballot measures. Vote on bond issues. Vote on county and state issues and initiatives.

Not voting is an abdication of civic responsibility. For the marginalized, it validates voicelessness. It is an act (by inaction) of self-disempowerment.

Know the issues. Know the candidates. Let your voice be heard.

Make sure you let your elected representatives know your views, even when there is a clear misalignment with theirs. The people who represent us need to hear from all of us—to know what all their constituents think, not just those who serve as an echo chamber. Call. E-mail. Write.

Understand that many organizations engaged in social

justice work monitor legislation and would be happy to keep you informed. I have served on the boards of directors of several nonprofits for whom legislative tracking became integral to their planning and programmatic work. The information, far from being secret, was collected so it could be shared broadly.

> **Accentuating Adage:** "Freedom isn't free. It shouldn't be a bragging point that 'Oh, I don't get involved in politics,' as if that makes someone cleaner. No, that makes you derelict of duty in a republic. Liars and panderers in government would have a much harder time of it if so many people didn't insist on their right to remain ignorant and blindly agreeable."[30]
>
> — BILL MAHER

**8. Delve into Diversity, Equity & Inclusion:** Practice introspection; self-discovery. Know yourself and your blind spots. Expand your circle. Seek out and explore diverse cultures and communities. Cultivate relationships that straddle lines of difference. Do the things you can do to be a positive example to others. A personal commitment to DEI and lived DEI experiences hone compassion and empathy.

Our shared humanity is the central message of DEI (and is explicitly called out in the "I"—inclusion). Our shared humanity lies at the heart of that national motto, *e pluribus unum* (in Latin, "from many, one"). Getting from "us and them" to "we" requires that each of us *know, care,* and *act.*

We need to know our history, warts and all, and know each panel of the quilt that is our diverse community. We need to care—to develop compassion and empathy for even the least among us. We need to act—to take steps toward inclusion and social justice in our own personal and institutional lives. Solutions must be both personal and political, a product of the heart and of the head: *tikkun hanefesh* (healing the soul) and *tikkun olam* (healing the world).

EXAMPLE: I work in the DEI space and have for well over twenty years. I still have to work at engaging with people who do not generally float in my waters.

I tend to be surrounded by people who are well-versed in DEI and are sensitive to language, microaggressions, and other verbal and non-verbal DEI cues. That is a subset, and almost certainly a minority, of the overall population.

I, too, harbor implicit biases—essentially, stereotypes derived from upbringing, education, media, and interpersonal interactions. We all do. I am at least somewhat self-aware, though, so I try to catch myself before acting on such biases.

Having an awareness of one's own fallibilities and vulnerabilities expands the space for humility, a valuable trait for those who work in the DEI space.

I strive to give people the benefit of the doubt; to extend grace. For example, when a man in one of my DEI workshops proclaimed, as often happens, "I don't see color. I'm colorblind," I resisted the temptation to bristle in disbelief or scowl in shock. What I and persons adept in the DEI space generally regard as a microaggression may simply be the product of ignorance. It may be a message perceived by the sender as well-intended or even self-congratulatory.

I paused and gently challenged the messenger: "That's interesting. I'm wondering if you know some take offense at what you just said, even though you intended none. If you don't see color and are colorblind, then you don't see me and the other people of color all around you. For us, that is neither a good nor a realistic thing. Our experiences, to a great degree, are grounded in color. Does that make sense?"

Well-intentioned people often lack self-awareness on matters of DEI. It may play out in a desire, whether conscious or not, to do *for* rather than *with*; to transplant rather than to grow; to lead rather than empower.

I recall a recent conversation with a white gentleman who had a plan for economic development in Tulsa's Black community, including the Greenwood District. I did not (and still do not) question his motives. When asked whether he had floated his concept in front of people who are part of the target community, he demurred. In his mind, this was a well-crafted, strategic initiative that could not fail. He consulted professionals—experts. Why would there be a need for consulting the targeted beneficiaries?

The man did not understand that one of the surest way to guarantee failure is paternalism. "For us, by us" resonates in the Black community. Ignore it at your own peril.

Delving into DEI enhances the likelihood of avoiding missteps and, if they are made, fashioning appropriate course corrections while maintaining goodwill.

> **Accentuating Adage:** "It is not our differences that divide us. It is our inability to recognize, accept, and celebrate those differences."[31]
>
> — AUDRE LORDE

**9. Pledge allegiance:** Pleas from groups hoping we will affix a simple signature to this petition or that pledge seem to appear nonstop. Why sign?

Remember the adage, "My word is my bond"? Sign because you commit to the object of the petition or pledge. Sign because you want to make a public statement about a matter of immense importance (at least to you). Sign because you want to set an example. Sign because you want to educate and motivate the community around a matter of significance. Sign because you want access to information that is likely to come from your affiliation with the cause that is the object of the petition or pledge.

Sign a pledge that is meaningful to you and commit to learning and doing more around the social justice issue that is the subject of the pledge. That said, your support of a cause with which you identify could significantly change the outcome for someone. This is one quick and easy act that could make a significant difference in the lives of others.

EXAMPLE: I am not a huge fan of petitions. They have their place, but I get more than my fair share of them. I see them mostly as irritants that unnecessarily clutter my e-mail inbox. That said, even though my inclination is to ignore them, on occasion one crosses my desk that is simply too important to ignore.

Examples of petition topics that appeal to me now include gun safety measures, DEI measures generally, and efforts to ensure inclusive curricula. Our collective voice on these matters may speak in ways our individual voices do not and cannot.

I even crafted a pledge for DEI that translates well into a petition:[32]

**I Believe** that every individual is precious and worthy; that every person is entitled to dignity and respect.

**I Believe** that the various dimensions of diversity, our differences, add richness and texture to the overarching commonalities that unite us.

**I Pledge** to . . .

- Embrace diversity, equity and inclusion by respecting such individual attributes as sex, gender identity, race, ethnicity, age, class, citizenship, marital status, sexual orientation, nationality, socioeconomic status, religion, physical ability, mental ability, and expression.
- Work for social justice on behalf of all people in order to create, nurture, and sustain an optimum quality of life for all.

- Choose my words carefully, refraining from the use of epithets and derogatory terms or statements that are harmful and disrespectful to others.
- Avoid reliance on stereotypes and instead leverage my experiences and interactions to better understand and embrace all people.
- Educate myself about cultures other than my own.
- Engage in and contribute to the diverse world around me by taking affirmative measures to foster inclusive environments in my community and work lives.
- Honor this pledge within my everyday life.

There are other ways to pledge allegiance. Show up at a peaceful rally or protest. Let your mind and body—your full presence—be your pledge.

Whether through words, resources (*e.g.*, money or other things of value), or our physical presence, pledging allegiance can make a powerful, positive difference.

**Accentuating Adage:** "There's always the danger that people will simply sign online petitions, the way they used to just mail in checks, and there's the greater possibility we'll just spend our whole lives staring at screens and never get anything done."[33]

— BILL MCKIBBEN

**10. Walk the walk:** It is not enough to speak the language of social justice. We must be part of a social justice culture. Stated differently, virtue signaling, a kind of superficial, public alignment with that perceived as good, right, or perhaps just trendy, is wholly insufficient.

Social justice begins at home. Practice self-reflection.

Involve your family, friends, and keep them informed and educated about social justice issues and human rights. Give them a global perspective and approach to life and living. Continue to educate yourself. Make a commitment to lifelong learning. Talk the talk and walk the walk. Authenticity matters.[34]

Edgar A. Guest, a popular writer and poet with the *Detroit Free Press* in the early-to-mid-20th century summed up the importance of setting an example—of personal integrity—in *Sermons We See*. The first two stanzas say it all:

I'd rather see a sermon than to hear one any day;
I'd rather one should walk with me than merely tell
the way.

The eye's a better pupil and more willing than the ear;
Fine counsel is confusing, but example's always clear;

And the best of all the preachers are the men who live
their creeds,
For to see good put in action is what everybody needs.

I soon can learn to do it if you'll let me see it done;
I can watch your hands in action, but your tongue too
fast may run.

And the lecture you deliver may be very wise and true;
But I'd rather get my lessons by observing what
you do.

For I might misunderstand you and the high advice
you give,
But there's no misunderstanding how you act and how
you live.[35]

EXAMPLE: For me, writing is a way of walking the walk. I advocate a more inclusive curriculum—the teaching of the marginalized histories of Black Americans and other persons of color. Saying that—speaking it—is necessary but not sufficient. My "doing" is chronicling some part of the history that ought to be taught and making it accessible to teachers—the people equipped and empowered to deliver it.

At a broader level, an arm of the Tulsa Regional Chamber of Commerce illustrates "walking the walk." The Chamber, an active player in the political dynamics in immediate post-Massacre Tulsa, has in recent years sought to be more engaged with and inclusive of the Black community and other marginalized groups. The Chamber has even adopted a DEI policy statement:

> In principle and practice, the Tulsa Regional Chamber believes diversity, equity and inclusion are essential to supporting our employees both in and outside the workplace.
>
> We believe when our people are at their best, our organization is at its best. We strive to foster an inclusive organizational culture for individuals to experience authentic, respectful interactions with colleagues and community leaders.
>
> We also support systems that increase economic access and mobility for underserved communities. We believe that celebrating diversity, championing equity and cultivating inclusion are critical to the economic vitality of the Tulsa region.[36]

"Mosaic," one concrete demonstration of the sincerity of the Chamber's DEI effort, launched about a decade ago. I helped initiate this new organization, which replaced a more traditional minority business outreach approach to whole-community engagement.

Mosaic's core message is that successful businesses learn to leverage diversity, foster equity, and promote inclusion. DEI affects all aspects of the business environment, including workforce attraction and retention, overall competitiveness, customer and client bases, and, ultimately, the bottom line.

Mosaic includes companies, nonprofits, and individuals who celebrate diversity, champion equity, and cultivate and celebrate inclusion within the regional business community. It is one example of putting the Chamber's professed commitment to DEI into operation.[37]

Walking the walk means being true to your professed principles. It means giving more than lip service to the social justice issues you claim to support. It means "keeping it real" by aligning words and deeds.

Take a moment to complete the following self-evaluation to see where you stand in terms of advancing social justice.

**Accentuating Adage:** "If you can't fly then run, if you can't run then walk, if you can't walk then crawl, but whatever you do you have to keep moving forward."[38]

— DR. MARTIN LUTHER KING, JR.

## Advancing Social Justice: Self-Reflection

Whether we fly, run, walk, or crawl, we can all advance social justice. We can go and grow from where we are. Where are you?

Each of us is at some stage of proficiency at addressing social justice challenges. Consider the 10 Ways We Can Advance Social Justice, then reflect on how many of those steps you have mastered.

Place a check mark in the circle next to each item you do

both regularly and well with respect to social justice issues. Determine your stage by summing up the number of checks and using the scale below.

- o **Speak truth.**
- o **Listen intently.**
- o **Show up.**
- o **Engage with your community.**
- o **Seek to serve.**
- o **Align with allies.**
- o **Play politics.**
- o **Delve into Diversity, Equity & Inclusion.**
- o **Pledge allegiance.**
- o **Walk the walk.**

**Self-rating:**

| | |
|---|---|
| **9 - 10:** | FLYER — Leading in matters of social justice. |
| **6 - 8:** | RUNNER — Advocating for social justice. |
| **3 - 5:** | WALKER — Engaging with others committed to social justice. |
| **1 - 2:** | CRAWLER — Becoming familiar with social justice concepts and issues. |

## 10 Ways We Can Advance Social Justice: Kids' Version

We tend to think of social justice as an adult concept, but we are all—children, too—part of the social justice fabric.

Children experience social justice in their homes and community. In the institutions that provide health and education. In the playground and streets of their community. In the neighbourhoods they live in. They are also actors and partners in promoting social justice through their concern and desire to uphold the rights of the most vulnerable children.[39]

Not only do children experience issues of social justice, they, too, have wisdom to share.

As a society and within our educational institutions, discussions about bias, diversity, discrimination, and social justice tend to happen in middle and high schools. We've somehow decided that little kids can't understand these complex topics, or we want to delay exposing them to injustices as long as possible (even though not all children have the luxury of being shielded from injustice).

However, young children have a keen awareness of and passion for fairness. They demand right over wrong, just over unjust. And they notice differences without apology or discomfort.[40]

Joseph Bojang, Digital Marketing & SEO Expert, shared the following Kids' Version with his children.

**1. Tell the truth.**
[Speak truth.]

**2. Listen to the world around you.**
[Listen intently.]

**3. Go to places and events that mean something to you.**
[Show up.]

**4. Do things *with* others.**
[Engage with your community.]

**5. Do things *for* others.**

[Seek to serve.]

## 6. Make friends and build connections.
[Align with allies.]

## 7. Tell grown-ups what you think.
[Play politics.]

## 8. Get to know various kinds of people.
[Delve into Diversity, Equity & Inclusion.]

## 9. Sign up to support and help with things that mean something to you.
[Pledge allegiance.]

## 10. Support what you say you believe in; do what you say you will do.
[Walk the walk.]

He was surprised with their reaction:

Having a discussion with my children regarding the 10 Ways We Can Advance Social Justice was enjoyable and illuminating. My initial goal for my seven-year-old and nine-year-old kids was to point out the complex and often concealed issues of social justice. They ended up educating me about how they were already thinking about these issues!

During our conversation, I realized they had a robust and informed awareness about the injustices they had noticed in their lives. Walking through the 10 Ways version for kids helped our family to learn from each other, build a vocabulary to better express our experiences, and understand that we all have stories to share.

Implementing the strategies introduced in this book is a terrific way to help kids walk through social justice issues, learn more about how they can be personally empowered, and exercise influence and impact on the world around them.[41]

We can all relate to social justice issues. Age-appropriate introspection, engagement, and advocacy matter.

> **Accentuating Adage:** "I am not bound to win, but I am bound to be true. I am not bound to succeed, but I am bound to live up to what light I have."[42]
>
> — ABRAHAM LINCOLN

---

FRAMING SOCIAL JUSTICE

---

"If you tremble with indignation at every injustice then you are a comrade of mine."[43]

— ERNESTO CHE GUEVARA

## POINTS TO PONDER

How will you stay motivated in your pursuit of social justice?

What are you willing to risk for social justice?

How will you measure success in the social justice arena?

# 6

## SOCIAL JUSTICE AND THE 1921 TULSA RACE MASSACRE: A CASE STUDY

"It is from the numberless diverse acts of courage and belief that human history is shaped. Each time a man stands up for an ideal or acts to improve the lot of others or strikes out against injustice, he sends forth a tiny ripple of hope, and crossing each other from a million different centers of energy and daring, those ripples build a current that can sweep down the mightiest walls of oppression and resistance."[1]

— ROBERT F. KENNEDY

*Williams Dreamland Theatre in Tulsa's Historic Greenwood District circa 1920; destruction landscape photo of Tulsa's Historic Greenwood District; photos courtesy of Greenwood Cultural Center.*

## Introduction

OKLAHOMA'S RICH HISTORY REFLECTS THE INTERSECTIONS OF Native American, African American, and European American cultures. The word "Oklahoma" means "land of the red people" in the Choctaw language. This history, though rife with oppression and conflict, reveals, more than anything else, a compelling narrative theme: the indomitable human spirit.

I take keen interest in the Black experience in Oklahoma, a long-neglected history that includes the successful economic and entrepreneurial sector, the Greenwood District, in Tulsa —"Black Wall Street"—and the devastating 1921 Tulsa Race Massacre that temporarily silenced its economic and entrepreneurial engines; Oklahoma City's renowned Black community, "Deep Deuce;" the Civil Rights Era activism of Clara Luper; voting rights controversies in the first half of the 20th century; the college desegregation effort of the 1940s led by Ada Lois Sipuel Fisher; the several dozen all-Black towns; Black cowboys; and Black Indians.

We cannot hide from the past, no matter how uncomfortable it may be. Rather, we must reconcile with our past now—

in the present—for the sake of our future. We must seek social justice.

One social justice issue looms particularly large. Until recently, Oklahomans in general and Tulsans in particular scarcely spoke of one of the nation's darkest moments: the horrific injustice perpetrated on Black Tulsans in 1921. Buried deep in Oklahomans' collective psyche, the Massacre, like a festering, septic wound, poisoned race relations for years to come. The legacy of that historical amnesia manifests itself in lingering mistrust, fear, and social distance between Black and white Tulsans.

A century-plus after the cataclysm, we have begun to think about reparation and reconciliation in earnest. How do we heal historical wounds? How do we bring our community together? What is our shared vision for the future? An honest examination of our past, intense introspection, and recognition of our shared humanity—our mutual interdependence—are basic predicates upon which the answers to these questions rest.

We ignore the lessons of our history at our own peril. Implicit in that truth is the necessity of remembrance—of recalling what transpired—to critically analyze and leverage the past for the sake of a better present and future. Though remembrance can be triggering, it is a risk we must bear.

Tulsa history presents an object lesson in the imperative of grappling with the past. The past is never fully in the past. The legacy of historical racial trauma still haunts us, but we are more conscious of its presence and better poised to confront it. Introspection, engagement, and advocacy are necessary elements of our journey from marginalization to magnificence—and from "us versus them" to "we."

The Tulsa massacre also tells us something about what can happen when parts of a community reject DEI and instead default to base prejudices and the systems employed to sustain and reinforce them.

Echoes of the Massacre still resound. The deep scars and fissures etched into the Tulsa community psyche will perhaps never be fully healed.

In many ways, the Massacre defiled and defined the city. That tragedy notwithstanding, the overarching narrative of its temporarily destroyed Black community, the Greenwood District, is rooted in human triumph.

The through-line connecting the most painful aspects of Tulsa history with so many other narratives of suffering (*e.g.*, chattel slavery, Indian Removal, Jim Crow, lynching, the Holocaust, and the Rwandan genocide) is the moral necessity that we—each of us—affirm the dignity and worth—the shared humanity—of all of us. Our failure to do so will ensure consequences that are swift, brutal, and enduring.

## HISTORICAL RACIAL TRAUMA, AMERICAN STYLE

Historical racial trauma generally refers to the mental and emotional injury caused by past encounters with racism and often triggered or exacerbated by ongoing racism.[2] Such trauma, particularly anti-Blackness borne of slavery, peonage, Jim Crow, "race riots," lynching, discrimination, and violence, both physical and psychological, is real, potent, and generation-spanning. It shaped our history and configured racial dynamics in ways that continue to hamstring our ability to leverage the power of our full potential.

Tulsa still grapples with the nuances and complexities of its slice of American history. Its experience is emblematic of so much other racial animus in American history and resonates beyond the city's boundaries. Others look to Tulsa for possibilities in terms of binding the wounds of hard history.

Healing our historical racial trauma requires us to: reflect on the historical context before, during, and after those fateful days more than 100 years ago, May 31 – June 1, 1921;

leverage our past for the sake of the present and future; and use our individual and collective agency—our capacity to be catalysts for positive change in race relations and ambassadors for the imperative of shared humanity (*i.e.*, the proposition that every person is entitled to dignity and respect).

Here is how Tulsa is grappling with the nuances and complexities of its slice of American history.

## TULSA'S HISTORIC GREENWOOD DISTRICT: "BLACK WALL STREET"

Post-Civil War land allotments awarded to the Freedmen of the Five Civilized Tribes, persons formerly enslaved by the Cherokee, Muscogee (Creek), Choctaw, Chickasaw, and Seminole, and descendants of those persons, helped fuel the economic engines of Black communities throughout Oklahoma, including the Greenwood District. Land ownership by these Freedmen and other "Black Indians," particularly in an agrarian economy, provided access to money for investment and consumption.

Early in the 20th century, Tulsa's Black community, several thousand in number[3], centered around Greenwood Avenue east of downtown and north of the Frisco Tracks, emerged as a nationally renowned entrepreneurial center, dubbed the "Negro Wall Street of America," later, simply "Black Wall Street." The Greenwood District's insular merchant and service economy rested on a foundation of necessity—a necessity that launched a Black business and commercial juggernaut.

A talented cadre of Black businesspersons and entrepreneurs plied their trades in rigidly segregated Tulsa, catering to a Black community shut out of the mainstream economy of the "Oil Capital of the World." The architects of the Greenwood District thus parlayed Tulsa's Jim Crow regime into an economic advantage.

This economic detour—the forced, race-based diversion of Black dollars away from the white community—allowed the thirty-five-square block Greenwood District to prosper. Dollars circulated repeatedly within the Black community.

Savvy entrepreneurs like Simon Berry developed their businesses around the needs of the community, "niche marketing" by today's standards. Berry operated a nickel-a-ride jitney service with his convertible Model-T Ford. He successfully operated a bus line that he sold to the city. He owned the Royal Hotel. He shuttled wealthy oilmen on a charter airline service he operated with his partner, James Lee Northington, Sr., a successful Black building contractor. Legend has it that Simon Berry earned as much as $500 a day in the early 1900s.

Prominent professionals like Dr. A.C. Jackson transcended, if only temporarily, the color line. Dr. Jackson, christened the most accomplished Negro surgeon in America by the Mayo brothers (of Mayo Clinic fame), treated white patients, too—remarkable given the rigid segregation that circumscribed all aspects of Tulsa life. Gunned down by a white teenager while surrendering at his residence, Dr. Jackson perished in the Massacre.

Industrious families like the Williams found economic success in multiple ventures. Loula and John Williams owned and operated several businesses, including Williams Dreamland Theatre, a confectionery, a rooming house, and a garage.

Capable, confident women like Mabel B. Little, proprietor of Little Rose Beauty Shop, operated thriving enterprises in the Greenwood District. Little, who hailed from the all-Black town of Boley, arrived in Tulsa in 1913.

Greenwood Avenue bustled on Thursday, the traditional "maid's day off." Black women, including those who worked in the homes of affluent white Tulsans, took advantage of the day's opportunity to "gussie up" and stroll along the busy thoroughfare. They did not go unnoticed.

Brilliant educators like E.W. Woods, principal of Booker T.

Washington High School for more than thirty years, beginning in 1913, gained respect and renown throughout the city. Woods arrived in the Tulsa area by foot from Memphis in answer to a call for "colored" teachers. He became known as "the quintessential Tulsan" for his preeminent leadership in the realm of public education. Tulsa's Convention Hall—the only facility large enough to accommodate the throngs of mourners—hosted Woods' 1948 funeral.

From movie theaters to professional offices, from grocery stores to schools, from beauty salons to shoeshine stands, the Greenwood District seemed to have it all. Black Wall Street teemed with business activity, and Greenwood Avenue, its vibrant hub, brimmed with all manner of commerce.

## THE 1921 TULSA RACE MASSACRE: TULSA'S SHAME

> The 1921 Tulsa Race Riot was the worst moment in Tulsa's history. Bigotry, fear and hatred overflowed in a murderous rampage. The public safety system that should have protected the city's black community failed completely, and the result was horrifying—a badge of shame that Tulsa will never completely live down.[4]

In early 20th century America, systemic, anti-Black racism ruled the day: urban (and some rural) "race riots;" lynching; and all manner of social, political, and economic maltreatment that affirmed white supremacy.

During the summer and fall of 1919 alone, America witnessed more than two dozen such events. James Weldon Johnson of the NAACP called the summer and fall of 1919 "Red Summer," red being a metaphor for the blood that flowed in the streets of places like New York, Philadelphia, Memphis, Chicago, Omaha, Washington, D.C., Longview (Texas), and Elaine (Arkansas).[5]

Equally horrifying, lynchings, acts of domestic racial

terrorism designed to effect white supremacy in the face of increasing Black assertiveness and amid swelling anti-Black backlash, took center stage. These brutal acts targeted and meted out ghastly vigilante violence, not simply to punish individuals, but also to send a message about the prevailing racial pecking order.

In Tulsa, fear and jealousy swelled within the white community as Black economic successes—including home, business, and land ownership—mounted and Black social and political aspirations rose.

Land lust set in. White business and railroad interests coveted Greenwood District land, nestled at the intersection of several rail lines, for a union terminal seen as integral for the rapidly growing "Oil Capital."

The KKK expanded in Tulsa and in the State of Oklahoma throughout the 1920s. The group boasted a roster that included a veritable who's who list of white society.

Media fanned the flames of racial unrest. Unbalanced, racially skewed coverage aroused racial tensions.

A chance encounter between two teenagers lit the fuse that ignited the Tulsa tinderbox and set the Greenwood District afire. The alleged assault on a white girl by a Black teen—an account later recanted by the girl herself—triggered unprecedented civil unrest. Propelled by inflammatory reporting in *The Tulsa Tribune*, resentment over Black economic achievement, and a racially hostile climate in general, mob rule held sway.

Authorities arrested the youth, Dick Rowland, and held him in a jail cell atop the courthouse. A swelling, gun-wielding white mob threatened to lynch him. Armed and defiant Black men, some newly emboldened after having risked life and limb for the United States of America in World War I, raced to Rowland's defense, trekking to the courthouse on two separate occasions.

Conflict ensued. A gun discharged. Chaos erupted. Soon,

thousands of weapon-toting white men, some deputized by local law enforcement, invaded, and then decimated, the Greenwood District.

Property damage to homes and businesses ran into the millions. Though the official death count stands at thirty-seven, hundreds of people likely died. Countless others were injured. Some fled Tulsa, never to return. The psychological toll on Tulsans in general, and Black Tulsans in particular, proved incalculable.

Initially dubbed the 1921 Tulsa Race Riot, but now generally referred to as the 1921 Tulsa Race Massacre, we might also dub this man-made calamity an assault, a disaster, a pogrom, a holocaust, a genocide, an ethnic cleansing, or any number of other ghastly descriptors. The Tulsa tragedy would remain a taboo topic for decades.

## BLACK WALL STREET RESURGENT

Bloodied but unbowed, Tulsa's Black citizens rebuilt their community. Within a year of the Massacre, the Greenwood District had been substantially rebuilt, with little thanks owing to leadership in the greater, white-controlled governmental and business sector.

By the early 1940s, the Greenwood District boasted more than two-hundred Black-owned businesses. Among the establishments that helped repopulate and reinvigorate Black Wall Street during the post-Massacre resurrection (*circa* 1935) were: Smith Tire Shop; Conway Grocery and Market; The Antlers Shoe Rebuilders; Flemmons & Seats Grocery, Market and Barbeque; Jones Drug Store; The Depression Club; Jackson Ambulance; Home Furniture; Neal Jewelry Co.; North End Garage; ABC Cleaners; Marie Griffin Beauty Shop; Benningfield's Electric Shoe Repair; Ligon's Grocery and Market; Little Rose Beauty Shop; Mann Brothers Grocery and Market; Lemons Bakery; Panama Cabs; Home Bottling

Company, Inc.; Archer Street Pleasure Parlor; Pat's Barbeque; Nicken's Sewing Shop; Security Life Insurance; Tom's Barber Shop; Attorney B.C. Franklin; Sunset Taxi Cab; Dr. A.G. Bacoats; E.L. Hairston, DDS; Inter-City Finance Corporation; Liberty Building and Loan Association; Docks Café; Busy Bee Café; Brown's Funeral Home; Claude Williams, Electrician; Hooker's Studio photography; Dixie Hotel; Small Hotel; Charles W. Graham, Violin Instructor; Hubbard Clinic; Bryant's Clinic; Delco Motor Service; *The Oklahoma Eagle* newspaper; Bailey's Pool Hall; W.B. Grayson real estate; Floryne Jackson, Notary Public; and The California Meat Market.

## A SECOND DECLINE

Integration, urban renewal, a new business climate, and the aging of the early Greenwood District founders caused the community to decline through the years, beginning in the 1960s, and continuing throughout the 1970s and early 1980s.

Most visible among the factors that precipitated the decline of the Greenwood District was the construction of Interstate 244, a cross-town expressway that passes through the heart of the Greenwood District, and U.S. 75 (Cherokee Expressway), which passes through the east side of the Greenwood District. These intrusions carved up the Black enclave, isolating its business center from the historically Black residential areas to the north and east.

Black Tulsans, and even the venerable *Tulsa World*, have begun to clamor for the relocation of the offending leg of Interstate 244 and the physical reunification of Tulsa's Historic Greenwood District.

We urge [our federal legislative delegation] to push for redesigning the downtown Interstate 244 corridor. It is an obvious injustice to the once thriving Black businesses and residents of Greenwood.

The district was going through an economic slump in 1967 when city officials, mostly white men, designed Interstate 244 to cut across the Greenwood district. That ensured that it would never be rebuilt.

Today, gravel and debris from vehicles on the interstate kicks up against the sole surviving building of the 1921 Tulsa Race Massacre—the Vernon AME Church. Developers have been frustrated by trying to work around the concrete beast.

The interstate is a physical and psychological barrier that has separated Black Tulsans from the rest of Tulsa.

As the federal government seeks to make right the harms by past infrastructure projects, we expect our elected officials to be at the table advocating for Greenwood.[6]

Tulsa's Black citizens held fast to hope. Preservation, restoration, and reconciliation became watchwords as healing history began to take center stage.

## THE 1921 TULSA RACE MASSACRE CENTENNIAL COMMISSION

The 1921 Tulsa Race Massacre Centennial Commission ("Centennial Commission"), formed in 2015 by State Senator Kevin Matthews[7], sought to educate all United States citizens about Tulsa's Historic Greenwood District, including details about storied "Black Wall Street" and the Massacre. In so doing, the Centennial Commission aimed to build social ties and unite communities.

The Centennial Commission's work fell into six categories which served as the basis for committees: Arts and Culture; Education; Bricks and Mortar; Economic Development; Commemoration; and Tourism. These pillars supported its ambitious agenda.

Each committee developed project goals. The Centennial Commission prioritized projects achievable by 2021, the Centennial year, realizing that initiatives designed to stimulate economic development logically follow bricks and mortar projects, and that relationship-building efforts—"road to racial reconciliation" projects—would be a continuous journey.

Central to the Centennial Commission's efforts was the creation of a world-class history center highlighting Tulsa's Historic Greenwood District. The museum-grade facility, Greenwood Rising—The Black Wall Street History Center, officially debuted in August 2021.

The overarching theme for Greenwood Rising, "The Human Spirit," speaks to the dignity of a people who turned trials, tribulations, and tragedy into triumph. The Centennial Commission's narrative commitments in portraying the story to the world, supported by input from community members, included:

- Celebrating the founders and the spirit of the Greenwood District in its different incarnations throughout history;
- Telling the full story — not just focusing on the Massacre;
- Including Greenwood District and City of Tulsa creation stories, and focusing on the different people groups and how they lived together;
- Referencing urban renewal (*aka*, "urban removal"), acknowledging it as another layer of racial oppression, replete with psychological, economic, and physical stresses on an already-marginalized community;
- Offering inspiration and hopefulness for future generations;
- Providing a space for discussion and consideration of "next steps;" and

- Creating, through writing and design, a facility that encourages reflection and repeat visitation, tapping into updatable content and changing gallery space.

Greenwood Rising features four galleries:

- Gallery #1 focuses on Black migration to and existence in Oklahoma and the remarkable human spirit endemic in the Greenwood District of the early 1900s;
- Gallery #2 focuses on the Massacre within the national context of the period, which included widespread racial violence in the form of lynching and "race riots" throughout the nation;
- Gallery #3 focuses on the resilience of Tulsa's Black community post-Massacre, which included the rebuilding of the Greenwood District as a thriving Black business community and its second decline in the 1960s and beyond occasioned by integration, urban renewal, and a confluence of other social and economic factors; and
- Gallery #4 focuses on the "Journey to Reconciliation," with space for dialogue to facilitate learning among school and other tour groups. This Gallery also includes a commitment space for patrons to acknowledge their individual agency in terms of addressing racial reconciliation, not just in Tulsa, but in the communities from which they hail.

Additional Centennial Commission projects included: construction of a Pathway to Hope—a walkway that reconnected the Greenwood District alongside the intersecting highway, Interstate 244, to the John Hope Franklin Reconciliation Park, complete with historical markers and tributes to

Greenwood District trailblazers; and renovation of Greenwood Cultural Center, a decades-old public venue and community programming hub.

I served as chair of the Centennial Commission Education Committee and local curator of Greenwood Rising, working closely with the world-renowned exhibit design firm, Local Projects, headquartered in New York City. Local Projects helped design the 911 Museum.

I witnessed firsthand the myriad ways the Centennial Commission made positive change, tapping all of the 10 ways to advance social justice previously referenced.

## BLACK WALL STREET: 10 WAYS WE CAN ADVANCE SOCIAL JUSTICE

Following are examples of how the Centennial Commission's work tracked with the 10 ways we can advance social justice.

### 1. Speak truth.

Throughout its work, the Centennial Commission focused on speaking truth to power. Senator Matthews went to great lengths to create a diverse, nonpartisan organization, including politicians. That body coalesced around the basic notion that the saga of Tulsa's Historic Greenwood District must be taught to both school children and the public at large. This fundamental, shared goal meant that certain truths long ignored would become front and center as the Centennial neared.

The coalition held together until late in the process. External events like the January 6, 2021, insurrection at the U.S. Capitol and the enactment of "anti-critical race theory" laws in Oklahoma and elsewhere tested its solidarity. Simply stated, critical race theory, which has its genesis in law school and university intellectual discourse, is a paradigm within which to speak forthrightly about the ways in which American history (specifically, our history around race, racism, and power) has affected and continues to shape society and its institutions.[8]

The insurrection and the opposition to the Presidential vote certification process that animated it, while roundly condemned initially, soon became politically partisan. With politicians on the Centennial Commission, tensions soon arose. The targeted, nationwide push against critical race theory, also partisan, heightened those tensions.

Oklahoma Governor Kevin Stitt signed House Bill 1775 into law on May 5, 2021. That measure aimed to hold sacrosanct a pristine view of American exceptionalism—a view of America as truth and light that rejects or, at a minimum, represses, falsity and darkness, past and present.

Generally speaking, HB 1775 prohibits public colleges and universities from requiring gender or sexual diversity training or counseling. It also prohibits, in public education at the primary and secondary levels, teaching, broadly speaking, about systemic racism or sexism—essentially, "hard history" that may make students feel discomfort.

The law explicitly excepts from its bans the teaching of concepts aligned with Oklahoma educational standards (*e.g.,* information about the Massacre). Even with this carve-out, critics pointed to the inherent chilling effect of the law on the incisive teaching of fraught history.[9] A 2022 *Tulsa World* editorial made the point thusly:

> HB 1775 is broadly and vaguely written, meaning enforcement is subjective.
>
> More significantly, this puts a chilling effect on teachers, who may ignore subjects on American race relations out of fear. This harms education quality, keeping students from information needed to be competitive in today's world.

Educators cannot teach American history without broaching the subject of race. What's more, teachers need to understand the differing backgrounds of their students before stepping into the classroom. It helps them be better at their jobs.[10]

Another Oklahoma newspaper, the *Stillwater News Press*, openly called for the repeal of HB 1775, warning: "The public school system is not a place where you can light a match and walk away. Some might think they are celebrating the removal of 'indoctrination,' but they're really celebrating the obstruction of critical thinkers."[11]

A couple of high-profile members resigned from the Centennial Commission as forces both within and without raised questions about their level of commitment, including support for teaching "hard history," the principle of "one person, one vote," and the defense of democracy. Remaining Centennial Commissioners weathered the storm, coalescing around and committed to their mission work.

The north-facing outside wall of Greenwood Rising sports a James Baldwin quote: "Not everything that is faced can be changed, but nothing can be changed until it is faced." Truth —acknowledging reality—matters.

## 2. Listen intently.

The Centennial Commission listened to a wide spectrum of community constituencies. Structurally, Senator Matthews built diversity into the composition of the body—not just racial and ethnic diversity, but viewpoint diversity and other dimensions of diversity, too. Elected officials, corporate leaders, laypersons, Massacre survivors, religious figures—all these were engaged at foundational and ongoing levels during the course of the work of the Centennial Commission.

Senator Matthews, in a 2019 letter to the editor prepared

for the *Tulsa World* and other print media, addressed the imperative of listening, but cautioned that to listen is not necessarily to agree or acquiesce.

We are a diverse Commission, populated with individuals of varying backgrounds and perspectives. Viewing that diversity as our strength allows us to openly discuss and debate 'Tulsa's Dirty Secret,' and invest our time, talent, and treasure to shed light on the past in ways that serve our community now and into the future.

We will create world-class cultural tourism and enhance economic development in the Greenwood District and surrounding areas. We will do this. We will not do this *perfectly*. Let's not let the perfect become the enemy of good. Progress is at stake.

As we work to create opportunities for what we can become, we must have the courage to endure the difficulties that accompany change. As an African American elected official, I am disturbed when I see and hear so much public discord about how we address the pain of the past and find solutions for the future. It is easy to criticize —to point out problems. The difficult part is offering up viable solutions.

Extreme division, name-calling, and blaming seldom yield much beyond more of the same: extreme division, name-calling and blaming.

I respect those inside and outside of my community and district who think differently. The best of us is on display when courageous leaders with differing perspectives come together in the spirit of cooperation for the good of the entire community.

The Commission has no power—and seeks no power— to stop anyone from criticizing, attacking, or otherwise working against it. That said, we seek to work with all those who are willing to meet us in the public square, with open minds, open hearts, and the courage to do the tough work, even when it's unpopular....[12]

From the outset, the Centennial Commission affirmatively sought out community voices by holding regular meetings and hosting community forums to sample community sentiment.

Not surprisingly, some criticized the Centennial Commission for not listening enough. Perhaps we did not. There is always more listening to be done.

The Centennial Commission listened when community members began lobbying for a change in nomenclature in describing the 1921 calamity. Historically known as the 1921 Tulsa Race Riot, vocal community members urged a transition from "riot" to "massacre" in all references to the event. We listened.

The Centennial Commission, originally called the "1921 Tulsa Race Riot Centennial Commission," deliberated on the matter, ultimately transitioning its name to the "1921 Tulsa Race Massacre Commission" consistent with the wishes of some of the most vocal members of the Black community. Our revised logo explicitly reflected the evolution.

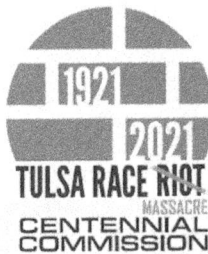

Another example of the apparent disconnect between the expressed will of some members of the community and the posture of the Centennial Commission centered on reparations. Some community members urged the Centennial Commission to advocate for cash reparations for Massacre survivors and their descendants. The Centennial Commission, while supportive of the concept of reparations, demurred, remaining mission-focused and continuing its specific work around education and entrepreneurship.

The Centennial Commission, aware of the imperative of listening to all voices in the community, issued the following statement on reparations.

We believe strongly in reparations. Our focus is on the larger scope of reparations, which means repairing past damages and making amends through acknowledgment, apology, and atonement. This process is central to racial reconciliation in Tulsa.

Survivors and descendants deserve remedy and reparation for the atrocities of 1921. The Centennial Commission's work toward reparations falls in restitution through advocacy for investment in education, infrastructure and economic development in North Tulsa. While far from comprehensive, Greenwood Rising and subsequent programming and initiatives will serve to hold space for visitors to learn about our past and present in order to work for a future in which these horrific events never occur again.

Reparations, as discussed in the 2001 final report of the Oklahoma Commission to Study the Tulsa Race Riot of 1921, involve compensation at the individual and community levels, and there are organizations and advocates working diligently for that purpose.

Reparations may take both individual and communal forms. Monetary damages are a type of individual reparations, and we believe that this is an important subject for discussion. Monetary investments in public spaces, public facilities, and economic initiatives are a type of communal reparations. These forms of reparations are complementary, not mutually exclusive. Both are important.

The Centennial Commission and Greenwood Rising, the

history center project it has led, seek to provide a platform where these issues can be discussed and moved forward in a meaningful manner.

Greenwood Rising honors the icons of Black Wall Street, memorializes the victims of the [M]assacre, and examines the lessons of the past to inspire meaningful, sustainable action in the present. This truth-telling and education for all is aimed at repairing lingering historical racial trauma—working toward restoration—and charting a new, vibrant, inclusive course for the future.

We support the work of others who are similarly committed to the pursuit of justice through reparations and racial reconciliation.[13]

The Centennial Commission made an earnest effort to listen to the voices of those willing to speak, distill what we heard, and act upon those inputs in ways we believed to be in the best interests of the community as a whole.

The effort was righteous. Whether it was "right" is, in the end, a subjective determination.

We listened, but was it enough? How much, though, is enough? How much listening is enough to those whose ideas and preferences are not implemented—those who do not feel listened to unless they win the argument?

## 3. Show up.

The Centennial Commission showed up for and with the Greenwood District. We sought and attained representation from nonprofits, churches, businesses, Massacre survivors, community leaders, and political actors.

Among those represented among the Centennial Commission leadership during various stages of its work: members of the United States Senate and House of Representatives; the Governor of Oklahoma; the Mayor of Tulsa; Tulsa County

Commissioners; Tulsa City Councilors; and members of the Oklahoma Senate and House of Representatives. Also present were representatives from: Indian Nations Council of Governments; North Tulsa 100; Greenwood Cultural Center; George Kaiser Family Foundation; Tulsa City-County Library; Metropolitan Baptist Church; John Hope Franklin Center for Reconciliation; Greenwood Chamber of Commerce; Tulsa Historical Society and Museum; Antioch Baptist Church; Morton Comprehensive Health Center; A Pocket Full of Hope, Inc.; University of Oklahoma; Oklahoma Historical Society; and the Oklahoma Department of Commerce.

Did we get the mix right? It depends on whom you ask.

## 4. Engage with your community.

The saga of Tulsa's Historic Greenwood District, legendary "Black Wall Street," is one replete with cycles of triumph (*e.g.*, its creation story; its post-Massacre resurrection), tragedy (*e.g.*, the Massacre; urban renewal and disinvestment), and transformation (*e.g.*, current development and investment; cultural tourism).

An angry white mob laid waste to Black Wall Street in 1921. Black Tulsans rebuilt it. Then, decades later, the robust closed economy that defined Black Wall Street faded as integration took hold. Paradoxically, integration, longed-for as a further step toward Black equality, proved detrimental, at least in terms of a short-term economic calculus. With this decline came the Tulsa Urban Renewal Authority's successful push to raze significant properties, ostensibly in an effort to eliminate blight. The Authority also elected to run a highway through the heart of the Greenwood District.

During and after the urban renewal phase, the State of Oklahoma acquired much of the area for use by various institutions of higher education. The city took significant portions of the neighborhood for flood control. The state ran Interstate

Highway I-244 through the heart of the Greenwood District, removing a substantial part of this once-bustling enclave.

In the wake of these devastating events, and in the midst of societal desegregation, the Greenwood District began to transform. Today, it is an integrated, multi-use, vibrant destination point, having leveraged its rich history in ways that encourage entrepreneurship, development, and tourism. Greenwood Rising is but one example.

Both the city and state acknowledge the rich, complex Black Wall Street narrative. Its lessons hold global significance. Still, too few people, including many Tulsans, know about this chapter of American history. The Centennial Commission worked to widen and deepen the shared understanding of that compelling story.

We engaged in and with the Greenwood District. Again, we sought to engage with the community throughout. We worked closely, with varying degrees of success, with key organizations like the Greenwood Cultural Center, the John Hope Franklin Center for Reconciliation, and the Greenwood Chamber of Commerce, both to forge collaboration and build trust.

We actively solicited financial "grassroots" stakeholders— individuals and small businesses from the community—to fund our work, particularly Greenwood Rising. We were adamant about extending an opportunity to ordinary Tulsans to participate in our transformational work. We encouraged, welcomed, and celebrated any and all financial gifts.

Not surprisingly, we raised most of the necessary funding from corporations and foundations. We also secured city and state funding.

We involved Greenwood District residents and others through community outreach efforts, including the Greenwood Art Project. Funded by a January 2018 Bloomberg Public Art Challenge grant, the one-million dollar Greenwood

Art Project consisted of a group of temporary public artworks celebrating and commemorating Black Wall Street.

Michael Bloomberg said, "Nearly 100 years after violence rocked Black Wall Street, and 50 years after a highway cut the neighborhood in half, the Greenwood Art Project responds with a message of unity and hope. The project will commemorate a community that once existed – and inspire people to envision a better, fairer future."[14]

Local artists participating in the Greenwood Art Project, with works spread throughout the city, spoke to the Greenwood District narrative and its centrality to truth-telling, community-building, and city unification.

As part of the Greenwood Art Project, MacArthur Fellow and Lead Artist Rick Lowe, with capable assistance from Project Manager Jerica Wortham, implemented social sculpture practices (*e.g.*, many ways of incorporating human activity as a means for structuring or shaping society or the environment) to close gaps and build bridges in Tulsa.

The success of the Greenwood Art Project rested heavily on the engagement of community members and local (Oklahoma) artists. As such, a series of engagement activities facilitated learning about Greenwood District history, providing context for the work that followed, and exploring present-day community issues to establish project relevance.

These at-least-quarterly engagement sessions over a two-year period were both entertaining and educational, offering optimal chances for collaboration and relationship-building across lines of difference. They simultaneously shaped the Greenwood Art Project in ways that celebrated and built community.

## 5. Seek to serve.

The Centennial Commission served the Greenwood District, primarily, and the wider Tulsa community, secondarily. That meant thinking about what would happen when we ceased operations. Our work elevated Greenwood District history, built a comprehensive history center (Greenwood Rising), leveraged cultural (heritage) tourism, and rekindled the Black Wall Street mindset. Maintaining and extending that work is important for the entire community.

Greenwood Rising is in some ways a successor in interest to the Centennial Commission in that it carries forward the educational mission, has become a cultural tourism focal point, and inspires the Black Wall Street mindset—the all-things-are-possible philosophy characteristic of the Black Wall Street icons.

## 6. Align with allies.

The Centennial Commission aligned with all manner of allies. Natural allies included organizations whose mission work centered on DEI and educational institutions.

Enduring partners included Tulsa Public Schools, Tulsa City-County Library, and the Oklahoma Center for Community and Justice. Without them, the accomplishments of the Centennial Commission would have been more difficult, fewer, and less sustainable. Nobody does it alone.

## 7. Play politics.

The Centennial Commission brought people together and bridged the partisan political divide. We found common ground on which the various political players could play, at least for much of the duration of the work. In so doing, we accessed additional funding from the city and state, respectively, for key projects like renovating the Greenwood Cultural Center and creating a statewide Black history website.

Despite its best intentions, the Centennial Commission could not wholly avoid the national partisan political tumult of the moment. Events at both the state and national levels, as previously noted, heightened tensions. Even still, maintaining a laser-like focus on our mission allowed us to weather the storm.

Perhaps the greatest challenge in this regard was the June 20, 2020, rally for Donald Trump's 2020 presidential re-election bid at the BOK Center in Tulsa. The COVID-19 pandemic raged during this period. Cases in Oklahoma spiked.

Critics and health officials warned against large public gatherings in confined indoor spaces, particularly given the lack of social distancing. Rally attendees explicitly assumed the risk of contracting COVID-19 as a condition of attendance.

Rally planners balked at the original scheduling of the event on June 19th, Juneteenth, now a federal holiday and long a date recognized in the Black community as emancipation day. That Tulsa was the site of the Massacre made rescheduling all the more imperative. Thus, June 20 became the new date.

In advance of the rally, the Centennial Commission issued a press release to reaffirm its commitment to social justice given the impending rally, seen by many as divisive and counterproductive. That document read, in part:

> The Centennial Commission embraces our shared humanity and the imperative of doing justice for all. Indeed, among the lessons to be learned from the Massacre is the folly that comes from dividing, marginalizing, and oppressing people based on race. Those lessons have yet to be fully embraced.

Both equality and equity remain elusive. Systemic racism is real.

All Tulsans, all Americans, are encouraged to drown out messages of derision and division with words and works that build people up; to take bold action in the fight against systemic racism and tear down the walls that have too long held us all back.[15]

In addition to the statement by and efforts of the Centennial Commission, Tulsans revived and reinvigorated the city's Juneteenth festival. As previously noted, a Bloomberg Philanthropies-funded public art initiative launched. Though not linked to or sparked by the rally, these efforts may be seen as implicitly responsive to it.

## 8. Delve into Diversity, Equity, & Inclusion.

Credible DEI efforts must confront the hard history that makes us uncomfortable. The Centennial Commission accepted the challenge early on and never wavered.

Greenwood Rising, the jewel in the crown of the Centennial Commission, tells a Tulsa-centric American story of the Black experience, both tragic and triumphal. That narrative cannot be told without reference to racial oppression—the American saga of slavery, lynching, Jim Crow, sharecropping, peonage, redlining, mass incarceration, and other forms of race-centered trauma.

Reckoning with our hard history in our communities requires that we:

- Incorporate hard history into community-building initiatives. For well over a decade, I have spoken to every class of my community leadership program, Leadership Tulsa, about Tulsa's Historic

Greenwood District and its role in and impact on community racial dynamics.

- Engage leaders from diverse segments of the community, sponsor community tours, view documentaries and news clips about the community's history, and facilitate dialogue sessions to hash out the too-often-avoided topics.
- Examine the role of hard history in shaping the institutions, structures, and systems that exist today —the same systems we rely on to deliver essential goods and services.
- Encourage engagement around the legacy of our hard history. Consider both conversations and actions that address race-based disparities in education, health care, employment, and criminal justice.
- Acknowledge the significance, both real and perceived, of demographic shifts (*i.e.*, the "browning" of America) on relative wealth, power, and privilege.
- Recognize that DEI is a moral and pragmatic imperative moored in our shared humanity. DEI, as previously stated, is both right and smart.

If we want to see meaningful, sustainable change in our communities, particularly in the realm of racial reconciliation, we must integrate our hard history into our work.

Our community history, including the difficult parts, is important. History exists whether or not we choose to acknowledge and address it.

Communities are not fashioned from whole cloth. We start with the torn fabric that was. We weave that into the material that is. We imagine the perfect garment that might be.

That is courage. That is leadership. That is the work of social justice.

## 9. Pledge allegiance.

The Centennial Commission crafted means by which people could personally commit to work toward racial reconciliation. As part of the Greenwood Rising experience, we built in a commitment space. Visitors, using an i-Pad or a cellphone via a QR Code, may type a short statement of personal commitment to racial reconciliation. That statement is then projected onto a brick on the wall among scores of other commitment statements.

We wanted patrons to do more than learn something about history. We wanted them to learn something about themselves—namely, that they have the agency through which to be difference-makers.

The commitment space seeks to cement that concept of agency by allowing visitors a means and an opportunity to publicly pledge specific ways in which they will be the change they want to see in the world. Reconciliation does not happen by accident.

## 10. Walk the walk.

The Centennial Commission encouraged people to do the work necessary to learn about and teach the history of the Greenwood District and to spark a Black Wall Street revitalization. Walking the walk is about integrity.

The last gallery of Greenwood Rising, the Journey to Reconciliation, provides prompts and is intended to serve as a connect-the-dots space. That is, how is this history I have just witnessed relevant today and going forward? How will I operationalize what I have learned in my life and through my choices?

## BLACK WALL STREET: STRATEGIC PLANNING

Addressing Tulsa's history around racial trauma lends itself to the strategy for addressing social issues, previously outlined and referenced below.

### 1. Establish ground rules for social justice conversations.

As noted, the four agreements for courageous conversations outlined previously (*i.e.*, stay engaged; speak your truth; experience discomfort; and expect and accept non-closure),[16] coupled with the ROPES values—respect, openness, participation, energy, and sensitivity—make up the four-by-five ground rules. These provide a sound basis for discussion of historical racial traumas like the hard history surrounding the Massacre.

### 2. Capture the context. Engage participants around DEI to ground them in the structural, institutional, and systemic bases of the social justice issues.

The context for the Massacre is both national and local. The national scene is painted with the "race riots" of the era, notably, the 1919 Red Summer events, and lynchings, not just in the South, but in places like Oklahoma, too. Locally, land lust, jealousy, the Klan, and the media are significant contributing contextual factors.

### 3. Define the particular social justice challenge to be considered using the "IRAC" paradigm.

An examination of the social justice issues related to the Massacre might proceed as follows.

- *Issue:* The most salient and enduring issue surrounding the Massacre is the status of Black Americans vis-à-vis the dominant culture.
- *Rule:* Laws and mores of the era condoned dehumanizing, second-class citizenship for Black people.
- *Analysis:* Systemic racism led to injustices, inequities, and atrocities.
- *Conclusion:* The challenge is to understand this history, acknowledge its legacy, dismantle the apparatus that reinforces it, and make efforts to repair the damage it caused.

## 4. Immerse yourself in the history of the social justice issue(s) at hand: How did we get here?

An outline of the saga of Tulsa's Historic Greenwood District has been presented. Books, articles, reports, and documentaries recount this history. In addition, Tulsa venues (*e.g.,* Greenwood Rising, the Greenwood Cultural Center, John Hope Franklin Reconciliation Park, and Tulsa Historical Society and Museum) present opportunities to explore and learn about Tulsa's Historic Greenwood District.

## 5. Consider ways to constructively engage around the issue(s).

Public forums, dialogue groups, community outreach, and curriculum-related activities are just a few ways to engage around this history. More broadly, constructive engagement might include exploring organizations and participating in initiatives focused on racial equity.

## 6. Identify existing and potential allies.

Potential allies include Massacre survivors/descendants, organizations engaged in work related to the Massacre or to social justice issues generally (*e.g.*, the NAACP, the ACLU, the Anti-Defamation League, and OCCJ), and churches.

## 7. Develop a strategic approach to addressing the issue(s) (*i.e.*, goals, timelines, responsible parties, and milestones)

Strategic planning, conducted by and for the group seeking to engage around the issue(s), creates space for new voices and visions. In the case of Tulsa's Historic Greenwood District, work related to restorative justice and community empowerment by community organizations is ongoing (*e.g.*, Greenwood Rising, John Hope Franklin Center for Reconciliation, Greenwood Cultural Center, and OCCJ).

## 8. Define success: What does it look like and how will it be measured, both qualitatively and quantitatively?

Begin with an end in mind: Define success and determine meaningful outcome measurement. For example, an award of monetary reparations is a sought-after measure of success with respect to the Massacre: direct payments to survivors and descendants of the Massacre by governmental entities (*i.e.*, the city and state).

Less frequently mentioned are indirect, communal remedies—targeted economic initiatives for the Greenwood District or African Americans in general that yield measurable outcomes (*e.g.*, growth in the number of Black-owned businesses in the Greenwood District, as measured by a simple count and comparison). Other such investments might include building facilities and institutions designed to elevate Tulsa's Historic Greenwood District and/or employ or otherwise enrich and advance Black Tulsans.

Economic *investments* in the affected community need not compete with direct *transfers* of cash to individuals. They might be pursued simultaneously or sequentially, depending on the circumstances.

Both transfers and investments constitute forms of reparations—measures taken to make amends and repair the present manifestations of damage that occurred in the past. Transfers, though, are more akin to legal damages: court-adjudicated monetary compensation awarded to persons who have suffered demonstrable legal harm occasioned by the wrongful conduct of another and who meet criteria under law for payment.[17] Damages rest on the direct connection between victim and perpetrator.

The entire city suffered on account of the Massacre, though the mob targeted the Black community, and that community experienced the overwhelming weight of the catastrophe. In recent years, efforts at memorializing this history, embedding it in the educational system, and advancing the Greenwood District economically (*i.e.*, investments) have come not chiefly from those who might bear legal responsibility for the Massacre, but from ordinary citizens, corporations, and philanthropists keen on creating a more welcoming, more inclusive city in the present.

In the educational realm, curriculum reform might be a measure of success—an example of the repair needed to mend a community hobbled by historical racial trauma. We might look at the increase in the numbers of schools that require teaching about Tulsa's Historic Greenwood District and the qualitative evaluation of that teaching.

Efforts to infuse this history into Oklahoma curricula began decades ago. The Oklahoma Education Department added the Massacre to the 2002 state academic standards, a list of legislatively sanctioned, mandated topics for public schools.

The addition, however, only obliquely referenced the Massacre, providing no clear direction on how to teach it. The mandate to schools: Teach the "evolution of race relations in Oklahoma" and "rising racial tensions," with the Massacre given by way of example or option. As such, schools might avoid it for any number of reasons.[18] Despite such vague direction, some educators created stunning learning experiences. One stands out.

In a May 23, 2021, Facebook post, Kenneth Joslin, Principal of Mayo Demonstration School in Tulsa and a former classroom teacher there, posted about a life-changing experience he and other teachers facilitated during the 2002 – 2003 school year. I recall reading a *Tulsa World* article about it. The post reminded me of how innovative, creative, and forward-thinking these educators were.

Third-, fourth-, and fifth-grade students were studying Tulsa's Historic Greenwood District, the city's segregated Black community. A four-person team of teachers gave them a special assignment: to build a scale model of Black Wall Street. The students toured the actual Greenwood District for inspiration. They constructed facades for the businesses and labeled the streets in their carefully constructed model.

They spent days working on the project and, upon completion, held a memorial celebration and invited parents. But that was not the end of the story.

After the memorial celebration, the teachers stayed behind. They doused the model with lighter fluid, set it on fire, and let it burn. They then took it back inside.

Returning the next day, the dismayed and distraught students could scarcely believe their eyes. Who destroyed their painstaking work and why?

Their teachers seized this teachable moment. This was

their way of introducing, in an unforgettable way, the Massacre.

They asked their disillusioned pupils to imagine what it must have felt like to lose real homes, real schools—real people.

Years later, former Mayo students said the project stands out as a powerful learning experience.

As a Black man who chaired the Education Committee for the 1921 Tulsa Race Massacre Centennial Commission, I know all Americans need such powerful and profound experiences to stoke compassion and empathy, particularly as we grapple with issues of race and historical racial trauma.[19]

The Centennial Commission, working in concert with the Oklahoma Education Department and other collaborators, helped expand academic standards on the Massacre in 2019. For the first time, the State required Oklahoma History classes to teach the destruction of the Greenwood District *and* its prominence as "Black Wall Street," a mecca of Black business and entrepreneurship.[20]

Our investments in curriculum reform paid off. This felt like success.

## BLACK WALL STREET: HEALING OUR HISTORY

One cannot heal from historical racial trauma without addressing the ongoing traumas we face. It is about addressing the past, attending to the present, and advancing an inclusive vision for the future. In Oklahoma and in Tulsa, we have begun that work. The following is a highlights reel, not an exhaustive listing, of some important steps toward social justice vis-à-vis the Massacre.

**1.** In 1997, the State Legislature created the Oklahoma Commission to Study the Tulsa Race Riot of 1921 to find facts about the Massacre and make recommendations regarding reparations. The Commission's final report in February 2001 meticulously documented the facts and made the following reparations recommendations:

- Cash payments to Massacre survivors [no action taken];
- Cash payments to heirs of survivors who could prove property loss [no action taken];
- The establishment of an educational scholarship fund [created on a limited basis];
- The establishment of economic re-development initiatives in the Greenwood District [The state created an unfunded economic development commission.]; and
- The creation of a substantial historical monument.

[The Oklahoma Legislature appropriated just over $2 million to assist in the construction of John Hope Franklin Reconciliation Park, a memorial to the Massacre and a tribute to Black Wall Street and Black history.][21]

**2.** Tulsa mayors, including the city's two female leaders, 36th mayor, Susan Savage (1992 – 2002), and 38th mayor, Kathy Taylor (2006 – 2009), and its current helmsman, G.T. Bynum, publicly apologized for the Massacre.

**3.** Prominent lawyers filed a much-heralded reparations lawsuit in 2003. The legal team that represented the Massacre survivor plaintiffs included Harvard Professor Charles Ogletree, famed O.J. Simpson attorney Johnnie Cochran, and Randall Robinson of TransAfrica. A federal court dismissed the case in 2004, based on the applicable statute of limitations.

NOTE: On September 1, 2020, Tulsa attorney Damario

Solomon-Simmons filed another reparations suit, this one based on an unusual application of public nuisance law, seeking civil damages for Massacre survivors, descendants, and others. After having previously eliminated some defendants and all plaintiffs save three living survivors, the Tulsa County District Court dismissed *Randle v. City of Tulsa,*[22] with prejudice (meaning the case may not be refiled) on July 7, 2023.[23]

**4.** The City of Tulsa launched police/community initiatives to build trust between the Tulsa Police Department and the various constituent communities it serves, including the Mayor's Police and Community Coalition ("MPACC"), begun in 2008 by Mayor Kathy Taylor.

**5.** In 2013, then-Police Chief Chuck Jordan issued a public apology on behalf of the Tulsa Police Department for its dereliction of duty during the Massacre.

**6.** The City of Tulsa, funded by the Rockefeller Foundation, identified and has begun to address race-based disparities that exist in all areas of well-being. The ongoing work began in 2017 with the mapping of equality indicators and the acknowledgement of gross disparities traceable to race. Using methodology developed by the City University of New York Institute for State and Local Governance, Tulsa's Equality Indicators Report uses fifty-four indicators equally distributed across six themes (services, public health, housing, education, economic opportunity, and justice) to measure and track the level of inequality in Tulsa. Each indicator is scored on a scale from 1 (full inequality) to 100 (full equality). Tulsa's overall score for 2021 was 39.2 out of 100, up from the baseline score of 38.28 in 2018. Though there is clearly immense work yet to be done, Tulsa Mayor G.T. Bynum expressed optimism: "I'm thankful to have these Indicators as a measure of where we were and where we need to be to our goals, many of which are now being realized through a shift from siloed approaches to community-driven solutions."[24]

**7.** On October 2, 2018, Tulsa Mayor G.T. Bynum announced his intention to investigate the prospect of mass graves long rumored to hold the bodies of Black Massacre victims. According to leading experts, the range of Massacre deaths is 100 – 300.

At the outset, Mayor Bynum explained a three-phase process:

> First, identifying if there are mass graves at all. And if there are, identifying what kind of mass grave it is. Is it a pauper's grave, or is it a true mass grave from the [M]assacre? And third, if it is a mass grave from the [M]assacre, then we want to do forensic examination on the bodies that are there to hopefully identify them and their causes of death.[25]

This initiative is ongoing. Healing is a process. That we have finally begun is cause for optimism.

**8.** Local organizations continue to facilitate a variety of educational initiatives aimed at building community and racial reconciliation, including those of the OCCJ (Anytown, Our Town, Different and the Same, Trialogue Series, Interfaith Tour, and the Youth Leadership Forum for Community Transformation), the YWCA ("Witnessing Whiteness" initiative), the John Hope Franklin Center for Reconciliation (Reconciliation Dinner and Symposium), and Tulsa Metropolitan Ministry (community/police dinner and dialogue sessions).

**9.** Economic gains continue to mount. On March 16, 2022, the Greenwood Chamber of Commerce opened a new Women's Business Center in the heart of the Greenwood

District to assist women-owned businesses and female entrepreneurs. Increasing numbers of Black-owned businesses call
the Greenwood District home.

**10.** 1921 Tulsa Race Massacre Centennial Commission (2015
– 2021), discussed previously, formed and chaired by Oklahoma Senator Kevin Matthews, focused on educating the
nation about Tulsa's efforts to address its historical racial
trauma, enhancing the Greenwood District for cultural
tourism, and rekindling the entrepreneurship so evident
during the heyday of Black Wall Street.

Through its Education Committee, the Centennial Commission sought to build public awareness through documentaries,
public service announcements, and a summer educational
institute for teachers. Working with internationally-acclaimed
exhibit design firm Local Projects in New York City, the
Centennial Commission created Greenwood Rising to tell the
Greenwood District story in an immersive, experiential way
and allows patrons to leverage history to address present-day
racial challenges.

The Tulsa Race Massacre Summer Teachers Institute
("Summer Institute"), a three-day workshop for Oklahoma
social studies teachers, included sessions by experts on topics
such as Massacre history, contemporary race relations in
Tulsa, and teaching difficult histories to diverse populations.
Participants took field trips to Tulsa's Historic Greenwood
District, the Greenwood Cultural Center, the John Hope
Franklin Center for Reconciliation, and the Tulsa Historical
Society & Museum.

Teachers enrolled in the Summer Institute accessed unparal-
leled opportunity to consult with experts on African American history and Tulsa's Historic Greenwood District,

including local historians, librarians, archivists, and community leaders.

The Centennial Commission also undertook other significant initiatives, including: building the Pathway to Hope, a connector linking key sites in Tulsa's Historic Greenwood District and elevating the icons who made Black Wall Street famous; promoting the Black Wall Street entrepreneurial mindset—the enterprising spirit around Black economic prowess and entrepreneurship—by expanding opportunity and options; and launching an Oklahoma Black History website, a clearinghouse for information on the Black presence and experience in Oklahoma, which is illustrative of broader Black history, replete with tales of triumph and tragedy, great and small, repeated across the decades.

**11.** On June 2, 2021, Tulsa City Council unanimously passed a nonbinding resolution to "acknowledge, apologize, and commit to making tangible amends for the racially motivated acts of violence perpetrated against Black Tulsans in Greenwood in 1921." Tulsa Mayor G.T. Bynum signed the document in April of 2022. Soon thereafter, the Council initiated a community-led process to gather evidence and provide input on what specific actions should be taken to address the racial disparities in North Tulsa, the historically Black community in the city.[26]

A *Tulsa World* editorial summed up the significance of the City's commitment to lead community discussions on Massacre redress:

**Editorial: 100 years after the Tulsa Race Massacre, the City Council apologizes**

The Tulsa City Council has apologized for the city's role in the 1921 race massacre.

'The members of the Tulsa City Council ... acknowledge, apologize, and commit to making tangible amends for the racially motivated acts of violence perpetrated against Black Tulsans in Greenwood in 1921,' the resolution passed Wednesday night says.

The council also apologized for its role in 'subsequent segregation, discriminatory practices and programs that led to inequities....'

Dozens, perhaps hundreds, were killed. Thirty-five blocks of the city, once the home to prosperity, were left in cinders. The city failed miserably to protect its Black citizens. At best it did not resist the murderous white mob that attacked the city's Greenwood section for two nights. At times it was complicit in the crime. The city resisted efforts to rebuild Greenwood and was part of the cover-up that followed.

One hundred years is a long time to wait for an apology for such a horrific civic failure, but only emphasizes that it was the right thing to do.

The debate leading to Wednesday's vote never centered on whether or not the city should apologize, which is healthy. The apology was overdue, everyone seemed to agree.

There have been arguments about what to do about it. Many who want cash reparations to survivors of the massacre were disappointed that the resolution didn't make a stronger statement on that point.

The council committed to a community-led process, beginning within the next six months, to evaluate the recommendations for reconciliation made in a 2001 legislatively commissioned task force that investigated the events of 1921. That is a coded reference to a public consideration of reparations to survivors and their descendants, the first two of several ranked recommendations for redress that came from the legislative study.

We understand the frustration of those who want more faster, but we also understand the value of a public discussion of the issue. If reparations are the right path to reconciliation, a public discourse can only bring a greater mandate, a greater success to the process.

We urge a process that listens respectfully, argues forcefully but fairly and is committed unflinchingly to justice.

We find wisdom in the words of City Councilor Vanessa Hall-Harper, a strong proponent of reparations.

The resolution 'is not a reparations proposal,' she said. 'It's about equity. The resolution is solely a vehicle to create infrastructures for good policies that will benefit Tulsa citizens who are and have been the most adversely affected from long-term systemic racism.'

We were gratified that the resolution passed unanimously. It says that the city is sorry for what it did and what it did not do in 1921. Even 100 years later, that's an important step. Mayor G.T. Bynum has said he will sign it, and he should.[27]

Tulsa must continue to grapple with its historical racial trauma. This is a work in progress and will likely remain so moving forward.

As part of healing our history, we should consider an appreciative inquiry approach—a look back for inspiration and example—for past positives that captivate and catalyze us in the present to fashion a more favorable future. The lessons and legacy of Black Wall Street offer a springboard from which to empower young men and women, promote self-development and self-sufficiency, and launch a new corps of Black business owners. Historical role models matter, not as replacements for such paragons in the here-and-now, but as supplements to them.

## THE BLACK WALL STREET MINDSET

"Black Wall Street" is as much a mindset, a construct built on promise and possibility, as it is a place. The rigors of race and the rigidities of residence no longer limit our horizons.

The ancestors, by precept and example, showed us what could be. Thus empowered, we, in tribute to them, should seize upon all our relative advantages to make it so.

Successful 21st century entrepreneurs and business leaders cannot be bound by the binary racial equation of the past. At the community, state, national, and global levels, racial and ethnic diversity abounds. Our challenge is figuring out ways to leverage that diversity to our optimal advantage.

DEI rests on the fundamental proposition that our shared humanity trumps all that might otherwise separate and divide us. How we treat the least among us will define our community. The hours spanning May 31 and June 1, 1921, in Tulsa provided a tragic, but illustrative, case study of man's inhumanity toward his fellow man.

We suffer trauma when events disturb our fantasy of a fair and just world. Sometimes, such events extend over time and generations. Such is the case with respect to the Massacre.

Greenwood District founders traced their lineage back to enslavement, sharecropping, and Jim Crow-style second-class citizenship in the Deep South. Escaping that racial crucible, they thought they had found their Promised Land in Indian Territory. However, they faced mirror-image Jim Crow segregation at Oklahoma statehood in 1907. Nonetheless, they built a flourishing commercial community against all imaginable odds.

Without doubt, there have been economic openings, better educational opportunities, and at least marginally enhanced social capital in the decades since those existential challenges. While not ubiquitous, open, honest dialogue, particularly around race, no longer occurs in mere whispers.

Still, persistent disparities in the social, economic, political, educational, and healthcare arenas, among others, offer overwhelming evidence that foundational fissures in the Tulsa community, caused and sustained by intergenerational traumas, require much more in the way of repair, much more investment by each of us.

Recovery from trauma presupposes an end to traumatic events, a protective cocoon of resilience, security, protections, and, finally, hope that a different narrative for the future may exist and persist.

The return of hope—of a widespread belief in fairness and justice—depends on the reduction and, ideally, the elimination, of trauma, some of which is revealed in literature today as "ACES"—Adverse Childhood Experiences—for our children.

We are community stewards. As such, we must marshal the resources necessary to heal the wounds of trauma that continue to shorten lives, disable otherwise healthy people, foster addictions, and, too often, create narratives of despair. When our dream becomes the shared narrative of brotherhood and sisterhood, of shared humanity, then we will have moved closer to "one Tulsa"—community unity.

The Centennial has passed. Now is the time to exhale, and then breathe freely, oxygenating our efforts on three fronts: (1) healing our history; (2) making an appreciative inquiry into our past; and (3) recommitting to DEI. If we do this, we will have honored the memory of one of our darkest days by illuminating it with a bright new light.

At the individual level, each of us can do simple things to move the needle on matters of race. Recall the three core actions needed to advance social justice: *introspection, engagement,* and *advocacy.* The following steps further those key actions:

- *Commit* to learning about people who are different from you in terms of the various dimensions of diversity (*e.g.*, race, ethnicity, gender, sexual orientation, class, religion, ideological inclination).

- *Devote* at least one day each month to thinking about how power, privilege, and prejudice affects you and might be affecting each person with whom you come in contact that day.
- *Meet* people representative of America's rich diversity by stepping out of your comfort zone and venturing into the unknown with an open heart and mind.
- *Counter* comments or actions that appear prejudicial, even if you are not the target of such comments or actions. Stand in the breach. Silence is complicity.
- *Initiate* a constructive dialogue on DEI within your workplace, school, neighborhood, or religious community. Dialogue is an essential initial step toward enhanced relations.
- *Support* organizations and institutions that promote diversity, equity, and inclusion. Get behind the solid work that is already being done.
- *Join* in a community project to reduce disparities in opportunity and wellbeing. Ongoing social justice efforts need support and joining in with others in projects also helps build the personal relationships that build the trust all communities need.
- *Insist* that organizations and institutions that teach us about our community accurately reflect the rich diversity of our nation. Do what you can to ensure that multiple voices and perspectives find their way into what is presented as American history. Oppose efforts to erode or eradicate teaching about "hard history"—about structural, institutional, and systemic dynamics that continue to shape and mold the social order.[28]

- *Visit* other areas of the city, region, country, and world that allow you to experience and engage with other cultures. We have much to learn with, from, and about others.
- *Advocate* for DEI in the groups to which you belong and over which you exert influence. Lead by example.

## FRAMING SOCIAL JUSTICE

"A generation which ignores history has no past—and no future."[29]

— ROBERT A. HEINLEIN

### POINTS TO PONDER

How is the Tulsa example symbolic of other instances of historical racial trauma?

What are the difficulties inherent in seeking to redress historical events?

How will you make the case that reparations in the broad sense of the word (*i.e.,* provisions designed to make amends or repair damage) ultimately benefit all people?

# CONCLUSION

"Human progress is neither automatic nor inevitable... Every step toward the goal of justice requires sacrifice, suffering, and struggle; the tireless exertions and passionate concern of dedicated individuals."[1]

— DR. MARTIN LUTHER KING, JR.

WHEN WE EMBRACE "WE" IN "WE THE PEOPLE"—WHEN WE live out the United States' motto *e pluribus unum*—we acknowledge our shared humanity, the *sine qua non* of social justice. With that acknowledgement comes reciprocal obligations that include compassion and empathy. If we share a common humanity, then we are obliged to walk the earth peaceably along paths that are shared with the many and varied co-travelers we will invariably encounter.

Civility, which accommodates the peaceable sharing of our social space, is in increasingly short supply. We seem to favor clashes over collaborations, raucousness over rationality, and pomposity over poise.

Television infotainment programs masquerade as "must

see" sources of news and information. Shrill hosts and combative, hyper-partisan guests, like gladiators, spar in verbal death matches.

The programs end. The lights go out. There we sit: intellectually numbed; ossified in our pre-program positions; and cursing the specter of compromise.

Reality shows, too often populated by shallow fame-seekers, encourage a "win-at-all-costs" mentality resulting in disrespectful, if not downright profane, behavior toward others. The essential calculation becomes: How might I *use you* to get what I want? Viewers learn that treating others as instrumentalities—as means to an end—helps them win, whether it be a game, a contest, or the ratings sweepstakes.

Social media misinforms as often as it informs. Miscreants manipulate it in ways that magnify and distort.

Politicians posture and pander, pretending to work on our behalf, but spending far too much time bashing political opponents and eschewing shared interests. These "tough" and "resolute" lawmakers' scorched earth tactics leave the peoples' business at best half-done.

What happened to civility? If we cannot respect one another, if we cannot see our shared humanity, if we cannot rally around the vast common ground we inhabit, we are lost. To paraphrase Dr. Martin Luther King, Jr., we are tied together in a single garment of destiny. That means our fates are linked, despite political and other differences. We choose to ignore that ultimate truth at our own peril. As we strive for social justice, for a more perfect union, we must also work for a more civil nation.

Achieving social justice is an aspirational pursuit—an ongoing journey that can be fraught with peril and disappointment. It is nonetheless a journey worth taking—a journey so many of us have no choice but to take. *Introspection, engagement,* and *advocacy* are essential stops along the way. Examine yourself. Plug in. Speak truth.

In the march toward social justice, equity is our North Star and equality our galaxy. We are propelled by both past and future—by history and vision. Temporary discomfort and sacrifice are the prices we pay for spanning new horizons.

Recall the earlier quote from Theodore Parker: "The arc of the moral universe is long, but it bends towards justice." I would perhaps modify the quote to account for the necessity of recognizing and acting upon our individual and collective agency: "The arc of the moral universe is long, *but with coura- geous effort, we may bend it* towards justice."

That sentiment perfectly captures the moral imperative for social justice, the necessity for action, and the hope we must maintain for those who embrace the challenge. A variant of an oft-repeated saying in Black culture reminds us: "Things ain't like they ought to be; things ain't like they gonna be; but thank God, things ain't like they was." Hope springs eternal.

Our world does not get better on its own. It gets better because we see its potential. It gets better because we appreciate its strengths and acknowledge its weaknesses. It gets better because we make it so through the pursuit of social justice.

We will encounter resistance along the road to social justice. Count on it. Bear in mind this warning: To the privileged, equality feels like oppression.

Moving toward social justice means someone must give up something (*i.e.*, privilege) so that the world works more fairly. The recalibration and rebalancing we must do will cause discomfort on the part of those surrendering unearned advantage. In anticipation, we need to maintain a mindset centered on abundance and fairness. It is possible both to expand the pie and slice it differently.

When we see ourselves in "the other," when we understand and appreciate our shared humanity, and when we commit to be difference-makers, all things are possible.

We must face our failures. We must face our fears. We must face our future.

## I CHOOSE LOVE

I choose inclusion.
I choose empathy.
**COMPASSION.**
Equality, dignity, diversity.
I CHOOSE COMMUNITY.
**KINDNESS. INTEGRITY.**
Honesty. Respect. I choose justice.
I choose facts. Peace. The planet.
I choose humanity.

## I CHOOSE LOVE

—author unknown

---

**FRAMING SOCIAL JUSTICE**

---

"Until the great mass of the people shall be filled with the sense of responsibility for each other's welfare, social justice can never be attained."[2]

— HELEN KELLER

# APPENDIX A

## Social Justice Organizations

The following is a partial listing of prominent social justice organizations.[1]

### Civil Rights Groups

**Action Center on Race and the Economy**
Provides research and communications infrastructure and strategic support for local organizations working on campaigns to win structural change by directly taking on the financial elite.

**American Association for Affirmative Action**
The association of professionals managing affirmative action, equal opportunity, diversity, and other human resource programs.

**Center for Media Justice**
Develops and teaches creative, effective, and participatory

communications and media activism strategies that support the fight for racial justice, economic equity, and human rights.

## Color of Change

The nation's largest online civil rights organization building grassroots political power for African Americans and working for social change for all people.

## Leadership Conference on Civil and Human Rights

A coalition of more than 200 diverse national organizations working to promote and protect the civil and human rights of all persons in the United States.

## National Fair Housing Alliance

Works to eliminate housing discrimination and to ensure equal housing opportunity for all people through leadership, education and outreach, membership services, public policy initiatives, advocacy, and enforcement.

## Political Research Associates

A research center that works to facilitate public understanding of the threat posed to human rights by oppressive and authoritarian right-wing movements in the United States.

## Race Forward

A public policy institute advancing racial justice through research, advocacy and journalism (it publishes *Colorlines*).

Civil Rights Constituency Groups

## A. Philip Randolph Institute

Works with Black trade unionists to fight for racial equality and economic justice.

## Japanese American Citizens League

Works to protect the rights of all segments of the Asian Pacific American community.

## League of United Latin American Citizens

Works to advance the economic condition, educational attainment, political influence, health, and civil rights of Hispanic Americans through community-based programs operating at more than 700 LULAC councils nationwide.

## NAACP

A civil rights organization (formerly, the National Association for the Advancement of Colored People) working for equity, political rights, and social inclusion by advancing policies and practices that expand human and civil rights, eliminate discrimination, and accelerate the well-being, education, and economic security of Black people and all persons of color.

## National Congress of American Indians

Works to secure the rights and benefits of Indians under treaties with the United States, give the public a better understanding of Indian people, and promote the common welfare of American Indians and Alaska Natives.

## National Council of Negro Women

A council composed of national African American women's organizations that lead, develop, and advocate for women of African descent as they support their families and communities.

## National Urban League

Works for racial equality for African Americans, fights institutional racism, and provides direct service to minorities in the areas of employment, housing, education, social welfare, health, law, consumer rights, and community and minority business development.

## OCA-Asian Pacific American Advocates

Works to advance the social, political, and economic well-being of Asian Pacific Americans (formerly, the Organization of Chinese Americans).

## Rainbow PUSH Coalition

A progressive organization of workers, women, and people of color founded by Rev. Jesse Jackson that fights for social change.

## Showing Up For Racial Justice

Through community organizing, mobilizing, and education, seeks to move white people to function as part of a multiracial majority for racial justice.

## Unidos

Works for civil rights and economic opportunities for Hispanic Americans and as a national umbrella organization for more than 300 formal affiliates in 41 states (formerly, National Council of La Raza (NCLR)).

Legal Defense of Civil Rights Groups

## Appleseed

A network of independent public interest law centers that use *pro bono* help to develop practical and lasting solutions to chronic injustices in public education, health care, child welfare, justice, and immigration.

## Asian Americans Advancing Justice

Works to advance the human and civil rights of Asian Americans through advocacy, public policy, public education, and litigation.

## Brennan Center for Justice

Uses scholarship, public education, and legal action to find innovative and practical solutions to intractable problems in the areas of democracy (voting), poverty, and criminal justice.

## Fisher, Sheehan & Colton

A small research and consulting firm that provides technical assistance to public and private organizations involved with the quest for social justice.

## Lawyers' Committee for Civil Rights Under Law

Marshals the *pro bono* resources of the bar for litigation, public policy advocacy, and other forms of service by lawyers to the cause of racial justice and economic opportunity.

## Mexican American Legal Defense and Educational Fund

Works to foster sound public policies, laws, and programs to safeguard the civil rights of the 40 million Latinos living in the United States and to empower the Latino community to fully participate in society.

## NAACP Legal Defense Fund

Uses advocacy and litigation to advance racial justice, focusing specifically on issues of education, voter protection, economic justice, and criminal justice.

## Southern Poverty Law Center

Combats hate, intolerance, and discrimination through education and litigation. The SPLC affiliate Learning for Justice (LFJ) serves the SPLC mission as a catalyst for racial justice in the South and beyond, working in partnership with communities to dismantle white supremacy, strengthen intersectional movements, and advance the human rights of all people. LFJ focuses its work with educators, students, caregivers, and communities in four areas: (1) Culture and Climate; (2) Curriculum and Instruction; (3) Leadership; and (4) Family and Community Engagement.

## Immigration Rights Groups

### America's Voice

Works to guarantee full labor, civil, and political rights for immigrants and their families.

### National Immigration Law Center

Dedicated to protecting and promoting the rights of low-income immigrants and their family members.

### National Immigration Project

A network of lawyers, law students, legal workers, and community advocates working to defend and expand the rights of all immigrants in the United States, regardless of legal status.

### United We Dream

An immigrant-youth-led network of 100,000 immigrant youth and allies and fifty-five affiliate organizations in twenty-six states that advocates for the dignity and fair treatment of immigrant youth and families, regardless of immigration status.

## Criminal Justice Groups

### Critical Resistance

Seeks to build an international movement to end the prison industrial complex by challenging the belief that caging and controlling people makes us safe.

**Grassroots Leadership**

Seeks to put an end to abuses of justice and the public trust by working to abolish for-profit private prisons.

**Innocence Project**

Works for the exoneration and release of factually-innocent inmates through post-conviction DNA testing and works to create a network of schools, organizations, and citizens that can effectively challenge wrongful convictions.

**Justice Policy Institute**

Works to enhance the public dialogue on incarceration through accessible research, public education, and communications advocacy with the goal of ending society's reliance on incarceration.

**Justice Strategies**

Promotes humane, effective approaches to criminal justice and immigration reform through rigorous analysis, high-quality research, and practical policy solutions.

**Prison Policy Initiative**

Documents the impact of mass incarceration on individuals, communities, and the national welfare, and produces accessible and innovative research to empower the public to participate in creating better criminal justice policy.

**Sentencing Project**

An independent source of criminal justice policy analysis, data, and program information for the public and policy makers.

Groups Challenging Capital Punishment

## Death Penalty Information Center

Provides the media and the public with analysis and information on issues concerning capital punishment.

## National Coalition to Abolish the Death Penalty

Provides information, advocates for public policy, and mobilizes and supports individuals and institutions that share an unconditional rejection of capital punishment.

Community Organizing Groups

## Center for Third World Organizing

A training and resource center that promotes and sustains direct-action organizing in communities of color to build a social justice movement led by people of color.

## Community Change

Works to build the power and capacity of low-income people, especially low-income people of color, to have a significant impact in improving their communities and the policies and institutions that affect their lives (formerly, the Center for Community Change).

## Gamaliel Foundation

A network of sixty affiliates representing multi-faith, multi-racial, church-going people who work on social justice campaigns.

## Direct Action and Research Training Center

A network of twenty-two grassroots, nonprofit, congregation-based community organizations working to win justice on issues facing their communities.

**Faith in Action**

A national network of faith-based community organizations working to increase access to health care, improve public schools, make neighborhoods safer, build affordable housing, redevelop communities, and revitalize democracy (formerly, PICO National Network).

**Industrial Areas Foundation**

A network of fifty-seven affiliates that build a political base within society's rich and complex third sector—voluntary institutions including religious congregations, labor locals, homeowner groups, recovery groups, parents' associations, settlement houses, immigrant societies, schools, and others—and then the leaders use that base to compete at times, to confront at times, and to cooperate at times with leaders in the public and private sectors.

**People's Action**

Coordinator of hundreds of local community organizations in 29 states fighting for community over greed, justice over racism, and people and planet over big corporations. Member organizations in People's Action include National People's Action (NPA), USAction, Campaign for America's Future (CAF), the Institute for America's Future, and the Center for Health Environment and Justice (CHEJ).

Disability Rights Groups

**American Association of People with Disabilities**

A cross-disability member organization dedicated to ensuring economic self-sufficiency and political empowerment for the more than 56 million Americans with disabilities.

**American Council of the Blind**

Strives to improve the well-being of all blind and visually

impaired people by elevating the social, economic, and cultural levels of blind people, improving educational and rehabilitation facilities and opportunities, and promoting greater understanding of blindness and the capabilities of blind people.

## Bazelon Center for Mental Health Law

A national legal advocate for people with mental disabilities.

## Disability Rights Advocates

Non-profit law firm dedicated to securing the civil rights of people with disabilities.

## Disability Rights Education and Defense Fund

Works to advance the civil and human rights of people with disabilities through legal advocacy, training, education, and public policy and legislative development.

## National Disability Rights Network

Works to create a society in which people with disabilities are afforded equality of opportunity and are able to fully participate by exercising choice and self-determination.

## The Arc

Promotes and protects the human rights of people with intellectual and developmental disabilities and actively supports their full inclusion and participation in the community throughout their lifetimes.

Elder Advocacy Groups

## AARP Public Policy Institute

Researchers and advocates on a wide variety of issues related to aging, especially health and long-term care, economic security, independent living, and consumer issues.

## Alliance for Retired Americans

A nationwide organization allied with the AFL-CIO and other partners working to ensure social and economic justice and full civil rights for all citizens, particularly focusing on retiree legislative and political issues.

## National Academy on an Aging Society

A policy institute that fosters critical thinking about the implications of an aging society.

Children Advocacy Groups

## Children's Defense Fund

Provides research, advocacy, public education, monitoring of federal agencies, assistance to state and local groups, and community organizing on a wide range of issues that affect children and youth, especially poor and minority children and those with disabilities.

## First Star

Works to change the U.S. child welfare system (child protective services, family courts, and foster care) from one of abuse and neglect to one of protection and support.

## Foundation for Child Development

Supports policy-relevant research about the factors that promote and support the optimal development of children and adolescents.

## National Head Start Association

Dedicated exclusively to meeting the needs of Head Start children and their families.

## Teen Talking Circles

Provides high school aged youth with weekly single-gender talking circles, called Daughterssisters and Brotherssons, and monthly mixed-gender circles, called GenderTalks and helps other groups start teen talking circles.

## The Annie E. Casey Foundation

A private charitable foundation dedicated to helping build better futures for disadvantaged children in the U.S.

Family Advocacy Groups

## Futures Without Violence

Develops innovative strategies to prevent domestic, dating, and sexual violence, stalking, and child abuse.

## MomsRising

Works to increase family economic security, to end discrimination against women and mothers, and to build a nation where both businesses and families can thrive by educating the public and mobilizing massive grassroots actions.

Feminist/Women's Liberation Groups

## American Association of University Women

Promotes education and equity for all women and girls, lifelong education, and positive societal change.

## Equal Rights Advocates

A national civil rights organization dedicated to protecting and expanding economic and educational access and opportunities for women and girls, specializing in advocating for the rights of women in minimum wage jobs, women of color, and immigrant women.

## Equality Now

Works to end violence and discrimination against women and girls around the world through the mobilization of public pressure, particularly on issues of rape, domestic violence, reproductive rights, trafficking, female genital mutilation, political participation, and gender discrimination.

## Feminist Majority

Works to promote women's equality, reproductive health, and nonviolence.

## Girls Inc.

Dedicated to inspiring all girls to be strong, smart, and bold, particularly those in high-risk, underserved areas.

## Institute for Women's Policy Research

A scientific research organization working to rectify the limited availability of policy relevant research on women's lives and to inform and simulate debate on issues of critical importance for women.

## Legal Momentum

Advances the rights of women and girls by using the power of the law and creating innovative public policy (formerly, the NOW Legal Defense and Education Fund).

## MS. Foundation for Women

Supports the efforts of women and girls to govern their own lives and influence the world around them by providing leadership, expertise, and financial support.

## National Organization for Women

An organization of feminist activists in the United States working to eliminate discrimination and harassment in the workplace, schools, the justice system, and all other sectors of society; secure abortion, birth control, and reproductive rights for all women; end all forms of violence against women; eradicate racism, sexism, and homophobia; and promote equality and justice in our society.

## National Partnership for Women and Families

Promotes fairness in the workplace, quality health care, and policies that help people meet the dual demands of work and family (formerly, the Women's Legal Defense Fund).

## National Women's Law Center

Fights for gender justice, taking on issues that are central to the lives of women and girls.

## National Coalition for Women and Girls in Education

Network of more than fifty organizations dedicated to improving educational opportunities for girls and women.

Lesbian, Gay, Bisexual, Transgender, and Queer (LGBTQ) Liberation Groups

## Gay & Lesbian Alliance Against Defamation

Dedicated to promoting and ensuring fair, accurate and inclusive representation of people and events in the media as a means of eliminating homophobia and discrimination based on gender identity and sexual orientation.

## Gay, Lesbian, and Straight Education Network

Strives to assure that each member of every school community is valued and respected regardless of sexual orientation or gender identity/expression.

## Human Rights Campaign

The largest national lesbian and gay political organization

working to ensure the basic equal rights of lesbian, gay, bisexual, and transgender people.

### Lambda Legal Defense and Education Fund

Works for full recognition of the civil rights of lesbians, gay men, bisexuals, transgender people, and those with HIV, through impact litigation, education, and public policy work.

### National Black Justice Coalition

Dedicated to the empowerment of Black lesbian, gay, bisexual, transgender, queer, and same-gender-loving people, including people living with HIV/AIDS.

### National Center for Lesbian Rights

Works to advance the civil and human rights of lesbian, gay, bisexual, and transgender people and their families through litigation, public policy advocacy, and public education.

### National LGBTQ Task Force

Advances full freedom, justice and equality for LGBTQ people. The first national lesbian, gay, bisexual, and transgender civil rights and advocacy organization and a leading voice for freedom, justice, and equality.

### National Youth Advocacy Coalition

Advocates for and with young people who are lesbian, gay, bisexual, transgender, or questioning in an effort to end discrimination against these youth and to ensure their physical and emotional well-being.

### OutRight Action International

Works to secure the full enjoyment of the human rights of all people and communities around the world subject to discrimination or abuse on the basis of sexual orientation or expression, gender identity or expression, and/or HIV status through advocacy, documentation, coalition building, public education, and technical assistance.

## PFLAG

Promotes the health and well-being of gay, lesbian, bisexual, and transgendered persons, their families, and friends through support to cope with an adverse society, education to enlighten an ill-informed public, and advocacy to end discrimination and to secure equal civil rights (formerly, the Federation of Parents and Friends of Lesbians and Gays).

## Soulforce

Works for freedom for lesbian, gay, bisexual, and transgender people from religious and political oppression through the practice of relentless nonviolent resistance.

## The Williams Institute on Sexual Orientation Law and Public Policy

Advances sexual orientation law and public policy through rigorous, independent research and scholarship, and disseminates it to judges, legislators, policy makers, media, and the public.

Family Planning Groups

## Advocates for Youth

Dedicated to creating programs and advocating for policies that help young people make informed and responsible decisions about their reproductive and sexual health.

## Catholics for Choice

Offers a voice for Catholics who believe that the Catholic tradition supports a woman's moral and legal right to follow her conscience in matters of sexuality and reproductive health.

## Ipas

Works globally to increase women's ability to exercise their sexual and reproductive rights and to reduce deaths and injuries of women from unsafe abortion.

## Medical Students for Choice

Works to persuade medical schools to include abortion as a part of the reproductive-health services curriculum to reverse the shortage of providers.

## NARAL Pro-Choice America

Fights to protect the right to choose — meaning having access to safe and legal abortion, effective contraceptive options, and quality reproductive health care (formerly, the National Abortion Rights Action League).

## National Latina Institute for Reproductive Justice

Builds Latina power to guarantee the fundamental human right to reproductive health, dignity, and justice.

## PAI

Champions policies that put women in charge of their reproductive health worldwide (formerly, Population Action International).

## Physicians for Reproductive Health

Works to enable concerned physicians to take a more active and visible role in support of universal reproductive health.

## Planned Parenthood

Operates health centers nationwide that provide high

quality, affordable reproductive health care and sexual health information to nearly five million women, men, and teens.

## Unite for Reproductive & Gender Equity

Engages young people in creating and leading the way to sexual and reproductive justice for all by providing training, field mobilization, and national leadership for a youth-driven agenda.[2]

# APPENDIX B

## Social Justice Issues

Following is a listing of some leading social justice issues in 2022.[1]

**Voting**

Organizations such as the National Association of Social Workers (NASW), the Anti-Defamation League (ADL), and the American Civil Liberties Union (ACLU) work to ensure voting is accessible to all United States citizens despite efforts to suppress and undermine the vote.

**Climate Change**

The threat that climate change poses to humanity is more evident than ever before. Climate change, however, can bring with it social challenges as well. It can put a strain on natural and economic resources and harm the overall well-being of all humanity. Climate change has also become a political issue and is a source of great division.

## Healthcare

An important aspect of social justice is the ability to have fair access to healthcare. There are still immense gaps in terms of coverage and access, especially where mental health issues are concerned.

## Refugee Crisis and Immigration

Conflict and climate change are two of the biggest contributors to mass migration. Famine and famine-like conditions are another key factor. Refugees face many social challenges, including language barriers, the inability to work legally, substandard living conditions (often informal tented settlements), gender-based violence, sexual assault, and post-traumatic stress syndrome. Access to education, healthcare, and economic opportunities is limited.

## Bodily Autonomy/Abortion

Bodily autonomy—the right to make decisions over one's own life and future—is about being empowered to make informed choices. Governments around the world have committed, in a variety of international agreements, to protecting autonomy. Respect for bodily autonomy is also a core tenet of international medical ethics.

Bodily autonomy is an ongoing, contentious issue in the United States. Some believe individuals should be able to choose what to do with their bodies, particularly (and most prominently) in the case of abortion. Others believe abortion is not (or not entirely) a pregnant individual's decision.

## Racial Injustice

Racial injustice impacts education, business, media, and daily life. Its long-term mental, physical, social, political, and economic consequences are as incalculable as they are inescapable. Examples abound.

The Covid-19 epidemic disproportionately affected racial

and ethnic groups, particularly Black, Latinx, and Native communities, who faced an increased risk of infection, major sickness, and death from the disease, as well as severe economic consequences. These gaps are associated with long-standing imbalances in health outcomes and access to care, education, employment, and economic position.

Some localities, as well as the state of California, trace these discrepancies to the heritage of slavery and examined various forms of restitution to correct them.

Private institutions like Harvard University have likewise acknowledged its ties to slavery and committed $100 million to implementing recommendations made by a committee charged with uncovering and revealing this troubling past.

> [O]ur recent progress must not obscure the reality of our past—or the continuing effects of the past on the present. The legacy of slavery, including the persistence of both overt and subtle discrimination against people of color, continues to influence the world in the form of disparities in education, health, wealth, income, social mobility, and almost any other metric we might use to measure equality. While Harvard does not bear exclusive responsibility for these injustices, and while many members of our community have worked hard to counteract them, Harvard benefited from and in some ways perpetuated practices that were profoundly immoral. Consequently, I believe we bear a moral responsibility to do what we can to address the persistent corrosive effects of those historical practices on individuals, on Harvard, and on our society.[2]

At the federal level, HR 40, a measure in Congress proposing the establishment of a commission to explore slavery's impact and develop reparations options, acquired extraordinary traction, with 196 House co-sponsors as of January 2021.[3]

The State of California has undertaken a collective soul-searching around the issue of chattel slavery and its legacy that is both informative and instructive for other states and for the nation. The California Task Force to Study and Develop Reparation Proposals for African Americans, a groundbreaking state government study of slavery, its effects throughout American history, and the compounding harms that the United States and California governments caused for African Americans, issued an interim report on June 1, 2022.

That document synthesizes relevant issues, including enslavement and government-sanctioned residential segregation, environmental injustices, and political disenfranchisement. Key findings from the interim report include:

- In order to maintain slavery, colonial and American governments adopted white supremacy beliefs and passed laws in order to maintain a system that stole the labor and intellect of people of African descent;
- In California, racial violence against African Americans began during slavery, continued through the 1920s, as groups like the Ku Klux Klan permeated local governments and police departments, and peaked after World War II, as African Americans attempted to move into white neighborhoods;
- Due to residential segregation and compared to white Americans, African Americans are more likely to live in worse quality housing and in neighborhoods that are polluted, with inadequate infrastructure;
- American government at all levels, including in California, has historically criminalized African Americans for the purposes of social control, and

to maintain an economy based on exploited Black labor; and

- Government laws and policies perpetuating badges of slavery have helped white Americans accumulate wealth, while erecting barriers which prevented African Americans from doing the same. These harms compounded over generations, resulting in an enormous gap in wealth between white and African Americans today in the nation and in California.[4]

Following the Covid-19 pandemic, many persons of Asian heritage faced violence and racial discrimination, particularly as anti-Asian slurs were used to describe the coronavirus.

## Gun Violence

Many consider gun violence to be a public health crisis in the United States. However, its impact can be felt across all aspects of life. The right to bear arms is protected by the Constitution. That said, no right is absolute. Citizens have proposed, with varying degrees of success, laws to curb gun violence by, for example, mandating background checks and banning certain types of weapons for civilian use.

## LGBTQ+ Treatment

The rights of Lesbian, Gay, Bisexual, Transgender, Queer, and other (LGBTQ+) has been a longstanding issue in the U.S. and around the world. Members of the LGBTQ+ community are still frequent victims of discrimination, harassment, and violence. They are often unable to equitably access educational, healthcare, economic, political, and other opportunities.

## Marital Rape

Marital rape is a type of sexual abuse in which sexual

activities are done on someone without their consent. In the United States alone, around 10 – 14 percent of married women have been raped by their husbands. One-third of women reported experiencing "unwanted sex" with their spouses. Marital rape is prohibited in all fifty states of the United States. Some governments around the world distinguish between marital and non-marital rape, subsequently categorizing them and dealing with them in separate manners.

### Child Abuse and Neglect

Thousands of youngsters in the United States face neglect and/or physical mistreatment, sexually and morally. According to the World Health Organization, up to one-quarter of adults were molested as children. These types of assaults have a lifetime of social and economic consequences, including psychological problems for these children as they grow into adults.

### Body Covering; Niqab

Countries including the United States have struggled with the problem of the Muslim veil, which comes in a variety of forms, including the body-covering and the niqab, which covers the face except for the eyes. The discussion encompasses freedom of religion, women's equality, secular values, stretching as far as terrorist worries.

The veil controversy is part of a larger discussion regarding multiculturalism, with many politicians arguing there should be a stronger effort to accommodate ethnic and religious minorities.

# APPENDIX C

**Black Wall Street: A Social Justice Plan**

*Exploring*
## LEADERSHIP, DEI & COMMUNITY
*Through*
# BLACK WALL STREET

## A SOCIAL JUSTICE ACTION PLAN
*Hannibal B. Johnson*

**Think globally. Act locally.**

"[Our] [h]istory, despite its wrenching pain cannot be unlived, [but] if faced with courage [it] need not be lived again."

— DR. MAYA ANGELOU

## Learning Objectives:

- Understanding Tulsa, Oklahoma, history of national and international significance—*Black Wall Street;*

- Appreciating the important leadership traits demonstrated in the historical setting of *Black Wall Street;*

- Applying the important leadership traits demonstrated in *Black Wall Street* history on a personal level; and

- Using *Black Wall Street* history as a springboard/catalyst for strategic, transformational community leadership.

## The Ghosts of Greenwood Past

### A Walk Down Black Wall Street

Early in the 20th century, the Black neighborhood in Tulsa—the "Greenwood District" or simply "Greenwood"—became a nationally renowned entrepreneurial center. Statesman and educator Booker T. Washington reportedly dubbed Greenwood Avenue, the nerve center of the community, "The Negro Wall Street" for its now-famous bustling business climate.

Legal segregation forced Black Tulsans to do business with one another. This economic detour—the diversion of Black dollars away from the white community—allowed for relative prosperity in the thirty-five square block Greenwood District. Dollars circulated repeatedly within the Black community. Greenwood's insular service economy rested on a foundation of necessity. This necessity, in turn, molded a talented cadre of Black businesspersons and entrepreneurs.

Savvy entrepreneurs like Simon Berry developed their businesses around the needs of the community, niche marketing by today's standards. Berry created a nickel-a-ride jitney service with his convertible Model-T Ford. He successfully operated a bus line that he ultimately sold to the City of Tulsa. He owned the Royal Hotel. He shuttled wealthy oil barons on a charter airline service he operated with his partner, James Lee Northington, Sr., a successful Black building contractor. Simon Berry reportedly earned as much as $500 a day in the early 1920s.

Prominent professionals like Dr. A.C. Jackson transcended, if only temporarily, the color line. Dr. Jackson, christened "the most able Negro surgeon in America" by the Mayo brothers (of Mayo Clinic fame), treated both Black and non-Black patients. Dr. Jackson died tragically in the 1921 Tulsa Race

Massacre, the worst of the so-called "race riots" in early 20th-century America. Gunned down by a white teenager while surrendering at his residence, Dr. Jackson, lacking medical attention, bled to death.

Industrious families like the Williams found economic success in multiple ventures. Loula and John Williams family owned and operated several businesses, including a theater, a confectionery, a rooming house, and a garage.

Capable, confident women like Mabel B. Little operated thriving beauty salons and other commercial establishments. They likewise added elegance and allure to the fabled thoroughfare. Greenwood Avenue bustled on Thursday, the traditional "maid's day off." Black women, many of whom worked in the homes of affluent white Tulsans, took advantage of the day's opportunity to "gussie up" and stroll down Greenwood way.

Brilliant educators like E.W. Woods, principal of Booker T. Washington High School for over 30 years, gained respect and renown throughout the city. Woods arrived in Tulsa by foot in 1913 from Memphis in answer to a call for "colored" teachers. He became known as "the quintessential Tulsan" for his preeminent leadership in the realm of public education. Tulsa Convention Hall—the only facility large enough to accommodate the throngs of mourners—hosted Woods' 1948 funeral.

From movie theaters to professional offices, from grocery stores to schools, from beauty salons to shoeshine shops, Greenwood had it all. So developed and refined was Greenwood Avenue, the heart of the Greenwood District, that many compared it favorably, if perhaps hyperbolically, to such historic streets as Beale Street in Memphis and State Street in Chicago.

In the late 1800s, Black boosters like E.P. McCabe touted Oklahoma, then divided into Indian Territory and Oklahoma Territory, as a virtual "promised land" for Black migrants from the South. McCabe dreamed of an all-Black state carved out of Oklahoma Territory.

Oklahoma attracted hordes of weary Southerners fleeing the oppression of the Jim Crow South and in search of full citizenship, land ownership, and economic opportunity. Though McCabe's "Black state" dream never materialized, Oklahoma boasted more than fifty all-Black towns throughout its history—more than any other state.

The promise of Oklahoma faded significantly at statehood in 1907. The new Oklahoma Legislature passed as its first measure Senate Bill Number 1. That law firmly ensconced segregation as the law of the land in Oklahoma. Jim Crow reigned.

The Greenwood originals parlayed Jim Crow into an economic advantage. They seized the opportunity to create a closed market system that defied Jim Crow's fundamental premise: Black incompetence and inferiority. The success of the Greenwood District, given the prevailing racial pecking order, could scarcely be tolerated, let alone embraced, by the larger community.

Fear and jealousy swelled over time. Black success, including home, business, and land ownership, caused increasing consternation and friction. Black World War I veterans, having tasted true freedom only on foreign soil, came back to America with heightened expectations. Valor and sacrifice in battle earned them the basic respect and human dignity so long denied in America—or so they thought. But, alas, America had not yet changed.

Stifling racial oppression and the intimidation and violence associated with it ruled the day. It was open season on Black Americans.

In 1919, there were some twenty-five major race riots in America. In 1921, at least fifty-seven Black Americans fell victim to lynchings. Despite these atrocities, the American government did little to protect her dusky denizens. Indeed, the United States Senate thrice failed to pass measures making lynching a federal offense.

In Tulsa, a seemingly random encounter between two teenagers lit the fuse that would set Greenwood afire. The alleged assault on a young white woman, seventeen-year-old Sarah Page, by a young Black man, nineteen-year-old Dick Rowland, triggered unprecedented civil unrest. That event became the immediate catalyst for the Massacre. Fueled by sensational reporting by *The Tulsa Tribune*, jealousy over Black economic success, and a racially hostile climate in general, mob rule held sway.

Authorities arrested Rowland. A white mob threatened to lynch him. Black men, determined to protect the teen from the rumored lynching, marched, armed, to the courthouse that held him. Law enforcement authorities asked them to retreat, assuring Dick's safety. They left. The lynch talk persisted.

A second group of men from the Greenwood District proceeded to the courthouse. The Black men exchanged words with the swelling group of white men gathered on the courthouse lawn. A gun discharged. Soon, thousands of weapon-wielding white men, some of them deputized by local law enforcement, invaded Greenwood.

In fewer than twenty-four hours, people, property, hopes, and dreams vanished. The Greenwood District burned to the ground. Property damage ran into the millions. Scores, if not hundreds, of people died. Many more were injured. Some Black Tulsans fled.

Ever courageous, the Greenwood District pioneers rebuilt the community from the ashes. Official Tulsa leadership hindered the rebuilding and rebirth of Greenwood, blaming Black citizens for their own plight, turning away charitable contributions for rebuilding, and creating reconstruction roadblocks. Some individuals and institutions in the greater Tulsa community stepped up, however, providing much needed assistance. The American Red Cross, called "Angels of Mercy" by many, provided stellar care—medical care, food, shelter, and clothing—for Massacre victims.

Lawyers Spears, Franklin & Chappelle provided legal assistance to Massacre victims. These Black lawyers lodged claims against the City of Tulsa and insurance companies for damage occasioned by the Massacre.

One of the lawyers, B.C. Franklin, successfully challenged the extension of a Tulsa fire ordinance that would have made rebuilding post-Massacre cost-prohibitive. Beyond that, they counseled and consoled Massacre victims and made urgent, nationwide appeals to Black individuals and institutions for assistance. Franklin, the father of famed historian John Hope Franklin, led the charge.

Mount Zion Baptist Church provides yet another example of the remarkable courage and determination of the people of post-Massacre Greenwood. The $75,000 church, only six weeks old when the Massacre broke out, had been built with the help of a $50,000 loan from a single individual. Rumors during the unrest that preceded the Massacre included a fictitious but persistent story that Mt. Zion housed a stash of arms for the looming racial conflict. The mob torched Mt. Zion during the Massacre, leaving nothing but a dirt floor basement.

Church members, still dazed by the devastation of the Massacre, made several key decisions. They elected to continue to meet, often in private homes. When presented with the option of extinguishing the $50,000 mortgage through bankruptcy, the church leadership balked. While the legal obligation could perhaps be eliminated, they felt a moral obligation to pay off the loan, even absent the building. Decades later, Mt. Zion did just that. The church paid off the loan and raised enough money to build a new structure. Mt. Zion remains a vital and vibrant part of Tulsa's Historic Greenwood District.

Remarkably, and in stunningly short order, the Greenwood District came alive once again, this time, bigger, bolder, and better. In 1925, Tulsa hosted the annual conference of the National Negro Business League. By 1942, more than 200 businesses called the Greenwood District home. The Greenwood story speaks to the triumph of the human spirit and to vaunted, timeless, universal virtues: vision, faith, determination, integrity, humility, compassion, and resilience.

Integration, urban renewal, a new business climate, and the aging of the early Greenwood pioneers caused the community to decline through the years, beginning in the 1960s, and continuing throughout the 1970s and early 1980s. Now, as the area is in the midst of a renaissance, the ghosts of Greenwood past loom large on the horizon.

**1. Describe one positive aspect of *Black Wall Street* history that stood out to you and/or held special significance for you.**

**2. What positive lessons in leadership, DEI, and community does the history surrounding *Black Wall Street* offer?**

## Personal Leadership Action Plan

Mindful of the lessons about leadership, DEI (diversity, equity, and inclusion), and community identified above, consider how you might apply those lessons to improve your community.[1] As you do so, recall the 10 ways to advance social justice:

1. Speak truth.
2. Listen intently.
3. Show up.
4. Engage with your community.
5. Seek to serve.
6. Align with allies.
7. Play politics.
8. Delve into Diversity, Equity & Inclusion.
9. Pledge allegiance.
10. Walk the walk.

Please take a few moments to respond to the following questions:

1. What action(s) do I want to take to challenge racism, discrimination, and inequality and/or to promote diversity, equity, and inclusion?

2. How will my action(s) impact the community?

3. What resources or materials do I need to realize my goal(s)?

4. How might I access those resources?

5. What specific behaviors or steps will be involved in securing those resources?

6. What is a realistic timeline for implementing this action plan?

7. What are the risks involved in implementing this action plan?

8. Is the contemplated action worth the risk entailed? (If not, go back to the first question or think through what might be done to minimize the perceived risk.)

9. What obstacles might I encounter?

10. What might I do to overcome these obstacles?

11. What are my support systems?

12. Where might I find additional support?

13. How will I measure success? How will I know if my personal leadership action plan was effective? (Consider whether slow, incremental change might sometimes represent "success.")

"Start where you are. Use what you have. Do what you can."

— ARTHUR ASHE

**Key Leadership Traits**

- Advocacy
- Awareness
- Collaboration
- Cooperation
- Compassion
- Creativity
- Curiosity
- Empathy
- Energy
- Engagement
- Enthusiasm
- Flexibility
- Focus
- Gratitude
- Hope
- Humility
- Humor
- Integrity
- Introspection
- Listening
- Optimism
- Passion
- Perseverance
- Persistence
- Resilience
- Respect
- Responsibility
- Self-Awareness
- Self-Discipline
- Vision

## The Lives We Touch

I was on a train on a rainy day. The train was slowing down to pull into a station. For some reason I became intent on watching the raindrops on the window. Two separate drops, pushed by the wind, merged into one for a moment and then divided again—each carrying with it a part of the other. Simply by the momentary touching, neither was what it had been before. And as each one went to touch other raindrops, it shared not only itself, but what it had gleaned from the other. I saw this metaphor many years ago and it is one of my most vivid memories. I realized then that we never touch people so lightly that we do not leave a trace. Our state of being matters to those around us, so we need to become conscious of what we unintentionally share so we can learn to share with intention.

— PEGGY TABOR MILLIN

# APPENDIX D

## Social Justice Reading Lists

- American Library Association, https://www.ala.org/alsc/publications-resources/book-lists/socialjustice (last visited September 2, 2022).

- Goodreads, https://www.goodreads.com/shelf/show/social-justice-reading-list (last visited September 2, 2022).

- Library Guides, https://libguides.midlandstech.edu/socialjusticereading (last visited September 2, 2022).

- Book Lists, https://socialjusticebooks.org/booklists/(last visited September 2, 2022).

- Book Riot, https://bookriot.com/a-social-justice-reading-list-for-those-who-want-to-rise-up/(last visited September 2, 2022).

- Learning for Justice, https://www.
learningforjustice.org/sites/default/files/2019-01/
TT-Reading-For-Social-Justice-Guide.pdf (last
visited September 2, 2022).

- Library Guides, https://libguides.umn.edu/c.php?
g=961505&p=8410614 (last visited September 2,
2022).

- The Institute for Gender, Race, Sexuality and
Social Justice (GRSJ) at the University of British
Columbia, https://grsj.arts.ubc.ca/wp-content/
uploads/sites/40/2022/02/2022_Social-Justice-
Reading-List-MLA.pdf (last visited September
2, 2022).

- Community of Literary Magazines and Presses,
Social Justice: A Reading List—Community of
Literary Magazines and Presses (last visited
September 3, 2022).

- Black Caucus of the American Library Association
and the Association for Library Service to
Children, a division of the American Library
Association, BCALA and ALSC Social Justice
Reading List | Association for Library Service to
Children (last visited September 3, 2022).

# ENDNOTES

## Acknowledgments

1. Dr. Martin Luther King, Jr., *Where Do We Go From Here?* (speech delivered at tenth annual session of the Southern Christian Leadership Conference, Atlanta, GA, August 16, 1967), available at Stanford University, The Martin Luther King, Jr., Research and Education Institute, https://kinginstitute.stanford.edu/where-do-we-go-here (last visited November 21, 2022).

## Foreword

1. Bianca Brosh, *Labor rights legend Delores Huerta: If you want change, here's how to get loud*, MSNBC.com, December 22, 2022, https://www.msnbc.com/know-your-value/out-of-office/labor-rights-legend-dolores-huerta-if-you-want-change-here-n1302120 (last visited December 27, 2022) (Delores Huerta speaking about ratification of the Equal Rights Amendment as part of the United States Constitution).

## Introduction

1. https://www.goodreads.com/quotes/98507-it-is-certain-in-any-case-that-ignorance-allied-with (last visited August 21, 2023).
2. https://quoteinvestigator.com/2012/11/15/arc-of-universe/ (last visited August 21, 2023).
3. *See* Joe R. Feagin, Racist America: Roots, Current Realities & Future Reparations (New York, New York: Routledge, 2000) (introduction).
4. *See, e.g.,* Federal Indian Boarding School Initiative Investigative Report, (recounting the horrors of the federal assimilation policy vis-à-vis Native Americans implemented through boarding school during much of the 20th century) (last visited May 18, 2022); Howard Zinn, A People's History of the United States, 3rd ed. (New York, NY: HarperCollins, 2003) (detailing the experiences of people of color in the United States).
5. *Confronting Anti-Black Racism Resource, Criminal Justice,* https://library.harvard.edu/confronting-anti-black-racism/criminal-justice (last visited October 27, 2022).
6. Stephanie Griffith, *Opinion: A look at one of the two athletes Obama said inspired him most,* CNN.com, June 27, 2022, https://www.cnn.com/2022/06/24/

opinions/citizen-ashe-tennis-racism-film-sport-edwards-griffith/ index.html (last visited June 29, 2022).

7. *Social Justice*, https://corporatefinanceinstitute.com/resources/knowl edge/other/social-justice/ (last visited May 10, 2022).

8. The George Kaiser Family Foundation ("GKFF"), a Tulsa-based philanthropy, illustrates the power of leading by example. GKFF's mission is to provide every child with an equal opportunity. Its four focus areas serve that mission and work toward social justice within the community: (1) parent engagement & early education; (2) health & family well-being; (3) vibrant & inclusive Tulsa; and (4) birth through eight strategy for Tulsa ("BEST"). GKFF supports, partners, collaborates, mentors, and otherwise engages with the various constituencies in the Tulsa community to create innovative, sustainable initiatives that reduce disparities and move toward equity. *See* http://www.gkff.org

9. *See, e.g.*, Hannibal B. Johnson, Black Wall Street 100: An American City Grapples With Its Historical Racial Trauma (Fort Worth, TX: Eakin Press, 2020). The Greenwood District, despite its successes, dealt with the kinds of discrimination in infrastructure and social services faced by other segregated Black communities, particularly in the American South. Water, sewage, and policing systems left much to be desired.

10. *Tulsa Equality Indicators*, https://csctulsa.org/tulsaei/ (last visited May 4, 2022).

11. This power-ceding approach—funding the priorities of communities of color as determined by persons of color—may address, at least partially, broadly expressed concerns about philanthropy some perceived as serving the interests of elites. Observers have noted that such philanthropy, guided by elites, may do good works, but functions primarily to maintain the status quo by tamping down discontent over economic disparities. *See, e.g.*, Edgar Villanueva, Decolonizing Wealth: Indigenous Wisdom to Heal Divides and Restore Balance (Oakland, CA: Berrett-Koehler Publishers, Inc., 2018); Anand Giridharadas, Winners Take All: The Elite Charade of Changing the World (New York, NY: Vintage Books, 2018).

12. Bill Major, in his role as Executive Director of the Anne and Henry Zarrow Foundation, the Maxine and Jack Zarrow Family Foundation, and the Zarrow Families Foundation, oversees the foundations' grant-making processes. He previously served almost two decades as CEO of LIFE Senior Services, the premier provider of home and community-based services for seniors in the Tulsa region. He concurrently served as CEO of Vintage Housing Inc., a nonprofit affiliate of LIFE Senior Services established in 1995 to develop affordable housing for low-and-moderate-income seniors in the Tulsa region. Prior to that, Major was the Founder and Executive Director of the Community Food Bank of Eastern Oklahoma, a position he held for almost ten years. *See* https://www.funderstogether.org/bill_major (last visited May 17, 2022).

13. BIPOC—Black, Indigenous, and People of Color—is a catchall. Critics argue that it presents an oversimplification of what is a complex web of historical, geographic, political, economic, and social experiences, only some of which are shared among the groups reflected in the label.

    Ideally, specificity should be the goal. If we mean Black people, we should simply say that and not default to the more general BIPOC. Our group experiences are varied and need to be acknowledged as such. That said, there are some interpersonal, intergroup dynamics that are similar in terms of the majority/minority dyad (*i.e.*, "white" versus "other"). There is value is exploring those common elements (*e.g.*, oppression, privilege, etc.) using some terminology for the mix that is the minority.

    It is not so much the acronym BIPOC that is problematic *per se*. Rather, it is the too-often clumsy, unthinking use of it in situations where specificity is required. Understanding nuance, context, and perspective is critical.

    It would be wise to engage with one another and have these more complex conversations about nomenclature in safe spaces. When it comes to language, we need to appreciate the multiplicity of possibilities, and not fixate on "the" answer/solution.

14. E-mail from Bill Major, May 6, 2022 (on file with author).

15. June 16, 2020, letter from Zarrow Families Foundation Trustees to Tulsans (on file with author).

16. In its inaugural grantmaking cycle in 2021, the Zarrow Commemoration Fund awarded more than $1M to community-based organizations, including grants for:

    —The facility renovation campaign for this North Tulsa summer and after-school program serving youth, predominantly of color, with physical fitness, tutoring, and activities that champion self-discipline. **REED COMMUNITY FOUNDATION**

    —Professional services to strengthen the legal and governance structure at this criminal justice advocacy effort led by survivors of mass incarceration who are predominantly women of color. **BLOCK BUILDERZ**

    —A trauma-informed student restorative justice program that will teach justice-involved youth in Tulsa County, predominantly teens of color, effective self-advocacy. **PHOENIX RISING ALTERNATIVE SCHOOL FOUNDATION**

    —Incubation of a new Community Development Financial Institution focused on affordable housing and governed by a majority board of color in partnership with North Tulsa leaders. **GREEN COUNTRY HABITAT FOR HUMANITY**

    —Production of an original music album performed entirely in the Cherokee language, aiming to correct the policies of white supremacy that attempted to eradicate the Cherokee language. **HORTON RECORDS**

    —Personal technology tools for the Fresh RX 'Food is Medicine' pilot program aiming to reduce uncontrolled diabetes in North Tulsa. **CROSSOVER COMMUNITY IMPACT**

—A new refrigerated truck to expand access to fresh, nutritious food for underserved LatinX residents in Tulsa. **LA COSECHA**

—Expansion of food delivery and healthcare prevention program in North Tulsa, to reduce hospitalizations and skilled nursing stays. **MEALS ON WHEELS OF METRO TULSA**

—Capacity building to expand community engagement work around individual wealth building and economic development initiatives. **MET CARES FOUNDATION**

—Safety and security repairs for low-income homes, contributing to improved housing values in North Tulsa neighborhoods. **REVITALIZE T-TOWN**

—Academically enriched daycare and after-school programs for students from North Tulsa neighborhoods. **TOUCH – TULSANS OPERATING IN UNITY CREATING HOPE**

—A creative after-school tech-training program targeting middle and high school students of color to develop a more inclusive tech ecosystem. **URBAN CODERS GUILD**

—Expanding distance learning, after-school tutoring, and STEM programs, plus new individual and family counseling and conflict resolution support. **TULSA DREAM CENTER**

—A new strategic plan focused on expanding resources for nutrition, financial stability, and workplace skills with on-site partners. **SOUTH PEORIA NEIGHBORHOOD CONNECTION**

—Healthcare services at this comprehensive medical clinic serving economically-disadvantaged Latinx patients. **COMMUNITY HEALTH CONNECTION**

—A multi-disciplinary media project that will center on Tulsa and the interwoven history, erasure, and racism that impacts the present-day lives of both Black and Native communities. **ILLUMINATIVE**

—A long-established North Tulsa, Black-led theatre program that stages and presents plays reflecting the African American experience. **THEATRE NORTH**

—Student tours to a new exhibit that explores the role of white supremacy in both the Jewish Holocaust and the 1921 Tulsa Race Massacre. **SHERWIN MILLER MUSEUM**

—Expansion of the Summer Y.E.S. Program, pairing students with Black business owners and professionals for internships and a business plan competition to grow long-term, generational wealth among Black youth. **TULSA COALITION OF 100 BLACK MEN**

—Programs at this high-performing and minority-led charter school, with a predominantly Latinx population. **TULSA HONOR ACADEMY**

Source: https://zarrow.org/commemorationfund/ (last visited May

3, 2022)

17. Casey Gwinn, J.D. and Chan Hellman, Ph.D., Hope Rising: How the Science of Hope Can Change Your Life (New York, New York: Morgan James Publishing, 2019).

18. https://www.goodreads.com/quotes/296639-there-must-exist-a-paradigm-a-practical-model-for-social (last visited August 21, 2023).

## 1. The Pillars of Social Justice: Introspection, Engagement & Advocacy

1. Excerpted from Maya Angelou, *On the Pulse of Morning*, https://poets.org/poem/pulse-morning (last visited August 21, 2023).

2. https://languages.oup.com/research/oxford-english-dictionary/(last visited April 20, 2022).

3. https://www.ala.org/advocacy/bbooks/frequentlychallengedbooks/top10 (listing top banned, challenged, and restricted books in libraries and schools for the last few years) (last visited June 8, 2022).

4. Following is a sample week's itinerary from one of my years as Anytown Director:

**Morning Discussion Themes**
Know Yourself
Know Your Family
Know Your Friends
Know Your Community
After Anytown
**Afternoon Workshops**
"Doing Democracy": Governance & Politics
Ethics
"Authenticity"
Discrimination Based on Sexual Orientation
We Are More Than What We Seem
**Religious Presentations**
Roman Catholicism
African-American Spiritual Traditions
Islam
Judaism
**Evening Programs**
Get Acquainted Evening
Prejudice & Discrimination
Gender Roles
Culture Night
Talent Night
Candlelight Ceremony
**Final Morning: After Anytown**

5. Julian Thomas attended Anytown in 1997. A graduate of Booker T. Washington High School (Tulsa, Oklahoma) and Northwestern University, he subsequently served on the Anytown staff, both as a counselor and an advisor. Julian is now a New York City-based actor.
6. Excerpted from a grant application submitted on behalf of Anytown in 2007 (on file with author).
7. When Moises Echeverria moved to Tulsa, Oklahoma, from Monterrey, Mexico at the age of 13, he spoke no English. He knew no one outside of his immediate family. He went on to become the first member of his family to attend college and complete an associate degree, a bachelor's degree, and a master's degree. He credits education with changing his life trajectory. *See* https://www.tulsacc.edu/about-us/stories/moises-echeverria-mhr (last visited May 17, 2022).
8. Rachel Weaver Smith, *Moises Echeverria: A quiet student turned vocal advocate now leads an organization that stands against bias, bigotry and racism*, Tulsa People, September 28, 2017, updated January 10, 2020 (last visited May 12, 2022).
9. Tulsa Changemakers, https://leadershiptulsa.org/programs/tulsachangemakers/ (last visited May 5, 2022).
10. Andrew Spector is a Co-Founder and former Program Director of Tulsa Changemakers, a youth leadership program that empowers young people to make meaningful change in their communities. He joined the Leadership Tulsa team as Program Manager in 2017 after completing two years of service with Teach For America, where he was a 6th grade teacher for Tulsa Public Schools. Andrew is originally from Bedford, Massachusetts and is a graduate of the Honors College at College of Charleston. At his graduation, Andrew received the college's highest honor, the Bishop Robert Smith Award, for his demonstrated leadership and academic excellence. Andrew has also served as Board Member for the Hillel of Northeastern Oklahoma and the Jewish Federation of Tulsa, tutored with Reading Partners, and been a member of Interfaith Youth Core's Alumni Speakers and Trainers Bureau. In 2018, Andrew was honored with ionOklahoma's NextGen Under 30 Award. *See* https://leadershiptulsa.org/staff/ (last visited May 17, 2022).
11. Jake Lerner is a Co-Founder of Tulsa Changemakers, a youth leadership development and action program that empowers young people to make meaningful change in their schools and communities. Jake is originally from Philadelphia, Pennsylvania and graduated from the University of Pennsylvania with a degree in Philosophy, Politics and Economics. In collaboration with the Wharton Social Impact Initiative, Jake co-created and facilitated social innovation and leadership identity workshops for high school students as well as undergraduates. He has also worked as a content advisor for Global Youth Empowerment's entrepreneurship boot camp in Dubai. Jake is a 2015 Teach For America Greater Tulsa Alumnus. In his free time, Jake plays basketball, writes poetry, and co-runs an

interfaith dialogue event for adults called Radical Amazement. *See* https://leadershiptulsa.org/staff/ (last visited May 17, 2022).

12. E-mail from Andrew Spector to author, May 11, 2022 (on file with author).

13. E-mail from Andrew Spector to author, May 5, 2022 (on file with author).

14. *See, e.g.,* Karen Ledford, *DEI's Intersection with Social Justice,* June 20, 2023, https://www.societyfordiversity.org/deis-intersection-with-social-justice (last visited December 12, 2023).

15. University of Pittsburg School of Public Health, *Pledge to Social Justice and Antiracism,* https://publichealth.pitt.edu/environmental-and-occupational-health/about/pledge-to-social-justice-and-antiracism (last visited March 4, 2022).

16. *Id.*

17. Merriam-Webster Dictionary, https://www.merriam-webster.com/words-at-play/woke-meaning-origin (last visited April 23, 2022).

18. Merriam-Webster Dictionary, https://www.merriam-webster.com/words-at-play/woke-meaning-origin (last visited April 23, 2022); *see also,* https://fee.org/articles/how-the-term-social-justice-warrior-became-an-insult/. The term "social justice warrior" underwent a similar transformation whereby what was once a complimentary phrase morphed, at least in some circles, into a derisive, sarcastic poke at those perceived as excessively passionate and smugly self-assured.

19. Maria Popova, *Albert Einstein's Little-Known Correspondence with W.E.B. Du Bois on Race and Racism,* kalamu.com/neogriot/2015/01/07/history-albert-einsteins-correspondence-with-w-e-b-du-bois/(last visited May 15, 2022) *(Einstein's original essay for The Crisis [W.E.B. Du Bois Papers, Special Collections and University Archives, University of Massachusetts Amherst Libraries]).*

It seems to be a universal fact that minorities, especially when their individuals are recognizable because of physical differences, are treated by majorities among whom they live as an inferior class. The tragic part of such a fate, however, lies not only in the automatically realized disadvantage suffered by these minorities in economic and social relations, but also in the fact that those who meet such treatment themselves for the most part acquiesce in the prejudiced estimate because of the suggestive influence of the majority, and come to regard people like themselves as inferior. This second and more important aspect of the evil can be met through closer union and conscious educational enlightenment among the minority, and so emancipation of the soul of the minority can be attained.

20. Former slave and noted statesman Frederick Douglass, in his "Composite Nation" speech in Boston in 1869, argued that diversity is, in essence, the United States' superpower, helping make it "the perfect illustration of the unit and dignity of the human family, that the world has ever seen." He continued:

[O]ur greatness and grandeur will be found in the faithful application of the principle of perfect civil equality to the people of all races and of all creeds, and to men of no creeds. We are not only bound to this position by our organic structure and by our revolutionary antecedents, but by the genius of our people. Gathered here, from all quarters of the globe by a common aspiration for rational liberty as against caste, divine right Governments and privileged classes, it would be unwise to be found fighting against ourselves and among ourselves; it would be madness to set up any one race above another, or one religion above another, or proscribe any on account of race color or creed [*sic*].

    *See*, https://www.blackpast.org/african-american-history/1867-fred erick-douglass-describes-composite-nation/ (last visited October 12, 2022).

21. *Adapted from* Efrosini Costa, *10 ways to promote social justice everyday* (February 20, 2017), https://www.mindfood.com/article/promote-social-justice/ (last visited January 21, 2022).

22. *Southern Poverty Law Center, Learning for Justice*, https://www.learningforjustice.org/magazine/teaching-about-kings-radical-approach-to-social-justice (last visited August 21, 2023).

# 2. Planning for Social Justice

1. https://www.brainyquote.com/quotes/booker_t_washington_133740 (last visited August 21, 2023).

2. United Nations World Day of Social Justice resolution, November 26, 2007, https://documents-dds-ny.un.org/doc/UNDOC/GEN/N07/464/37/PDF/N0746437.pdf?OpenElement (last visited March 17, 2022).

3. World Day of Social Justice, https://worlddayofsocialjustice.com/ (last visited March 17, 2022).

4. Justice Jose P. Laurel, *Maximo Calalang v. A.D. Williams*, 70 Phil. 726 (1940), https://www.chanrobles.com/cralaw/1940decemberdecisions.php?id=237 (last visited March 28, 2022); *see also* https://twt.com.ph/2018/04/what-is-social-justice-according-to-justice-jose-laurel/ (last visited March 28, 2022). José Paciano Laurel y García (March 9, 1891 – November 6, 1959) was a Filipino politician and judge who served as the president of the Japanese-occupied Second Philippine Republic, a puppet state during World War II, from 1943 to 1945.

5. *Social Justice: A political and philosophical theory that focuses on the concept of fairness in relations between individuals in society*, Corporate Finance Institute, May 8, 2022, https://corporatefinanceinstitute.com/resources/knowl edge/other/social-justice/ (last visited August 16, 2022).

6. https://www.archives.gov/founding-docs/declaration (last visited March 18, 2022).

7. *See* Kipton Jensen and Preston King, *Beloved Community: Martin Luther King, Howard Thurman, and Josiah Royce*, AMITY: The Journal of Friendship

Studies (2017), 4(1): 15–31, https://amityjournal.leeds.ac.uk/issues/volume-4/beloved-community/ (last visited September 2, 2022):

ABSTRACT

Martin Luther King's primary emphasis was upon 'beloved community,' a phrase he borrowed from Royce [American philosopher Josiah Royce, 1855 – 1916], but an idea that he shared with St. Augustine. Theories of the state tend to focus upon division, in which one stratum dominates another or others. King's context is the US in the segregated South—a region whose internal divisions sharply instantiate the idea of the state as an unequal hierarchy of dominance. King's appeal was less to end black subjugation than to end subjugation as such. Hence King was called by some a 'dreamer,' given his background commitment to equality and community, ideals taking marginal precedence over his foreground commitment to liberty and autonomy....

8. *The 8ᵗʰ Principle of Unitarian Universalism*, https://www.8thprincipleuu.org/what-is-beloved-community (last visited March 15, 2022).

9. For others, thoughts of a "Beloved Community" may have surfaced during the COVID-19 pandemic or in the wake of the killing of George Floyd.

10. Cassie Miller and Rachel Carroll Rivas, *The Year in Hate and Extremism 2021*, The Year in Hate & Extremism 2021 (Montgomery, AL: Southern Poverty Law Center, 2022), at 17.

11. James Luther Adams, *Theological Bases of Social Action*, in On Being Human Religiously, edited by Max L. Stackhouse (Boston: Unitarian Universalist Association, 1976), at 114.

12. *See generally, Social Justice: A political and philosophical theory that focuses on the concept of fairness in relations between individuals in society*, Corporate Finance Institute, May 8, 2022, https://corporatefinanceinstitute.com/resources/knowledge/other/social-justice/ (last visited August 16, 2022); Winslade, John M. (2015) *What is Social Justice? Opening a Discussion*, Wisdom in Education: Vol. 5 : Issue 1 , Article 3 available at: https://scholarworks.lib.csusb.edu/wie/vol5/iss1/3 (last visited August 16, 2022).

13. https://www.anothermag.com/design-living/12607/angela-davis-quotes-on-freedom-juneteenth-black-lives-matter-movement (last visited August 21, 2023).

## 3. Seeking Social Justice: A Strategic Approach

1. https://www.brainyquote.com/quotes/marian_wright_edelman_400723 (last visited August 21, 2023).

2. Another process, this one centered primarily around cultural competence, is that explored by Jonnie Seay Lane in a Counseling Today article entitled, *An eight-step process for implementing social justice and advocacy interven-*

*tions,* https://ct.counseling.org/2017/06/eight-step-process-implement
ing-social-justice-advocacy-interventions/(last visited April 4, 2022):

**Steps for implementing social justice and advocacy inter-
ventions:**

**Step One:** Identify the need(s) of your client or population.

**Step Two:** Decide in which layer(s) your client's or population's
needs are represented (*e.g.*, a client seeking assistance for solving commu-
nicating issues with a co-worker has needs in the interpersonal layer).

**Step Three:** Review the interventions from the appropriate layer in
the model and ask yourself the following questions: In what ways are my
client's or population's needs being (or not being) met?; Which interventions in this layer relate to my client's or population's current problem
areas?; and How am I doing as a counselor with each intervention?

**Step Four:** Communicate your thoughts with others (co-workers,
supervisors, collateral sources and, most importantly, your client). Gain
insight and perspective from their understanding of the nature, intensity,
diagnosis and prognosis of the problem.

**Step Five:** Decide where effort devoted to a specific intervention will
adequately address the need(s) identified in Step One.

**Step Six:** Develop a strategy for implementing the intervention. Ask
yourself the following questions: Who takes ownership of the intervention?; What is my role in this intervention?; Who else is involved in this
intervention?; Who or where do I need to elicit assistance from?; What
are the potential outcomes (pros/cons) of implementing this intervention?; What will I need to do to prepare for the outcome of implementing this intervention?; and What is the timeline for implementing
this strategy?

**Step Seven:** Evaluate the outcome: Did you what you hoped you
would?; Talk with your client(s). What is his or her perspective in terms
of advocacy and social justice?; If you have a formal multicultural counseling assessment or questionnaire, employ that before and after implementation.

**Step Eight:** Adjust, as necessary, or create a "maintenance plan" for
this intervention. Ask the following questions: How will I ensure that this
competency remains as is?; and How often will I go back and evaluate
the state of this intervention?

3. *See, e.g., 12 charts show how racial disparities persists across wealth, health, education and beyond,* https://www.usatoday.com/in-depth/news/2020/06/18/
12-charts-racial-disparities-persist-across-wealth-health-and-beyond/
3201129001/ (last visited April 12, 2022).

4. Glenn E. Singleton and Curtis Linton, Courageous Conversations About
Race: A Field Guide for Achieving Equity in Schools (Thousand Oaks,
CA: Sage Publications, Inc., 2005).

5. Black Lives Matter, https://blacklivesmatter.com/ (last visited March 23,
2022).

6. *Id.*

7. Bret Turner, *Teaching Kindness Isn't Enough: Teaching kindness is a staple of elementary practice, but that isn't the same as teaching justice*, Learning for Justice (Issue 63, Fall 2019), https://www.learningforjustice.org/magazine/fall-2019/teaching-kindness-isnt-enough (last visited August 24, 2022).
8. https://www.goodreads.com/author/quotes/95227.Ha_Joon_Chang (last visited August 21, 2023).

## 4. Social Justice and Diversity, Equity & Inclusion

1. *Teambuilding.com*, https://teambuilding.com/blog/diversity-and-inclusion-quotes (last visited August 21, 2
2. https://www.socialventurepartners.org/wp-content/uploads/2018/01/Problem-with-Equity-vs-Equality-Graphic.pdf (last visited March 18, 2022).
3. Similarly, broadly shared notions of fairness have traditionally dictated that male and female athletes compete in same-gender contests to account for biological differences. Emerging issues regarding gender identity have added depth and complexity to this discussion around equity.
4. Source: Adapted from Lee Gardenswartz, Ph.D. & Anita Rowe, Ph.D., From Diverse Teams at Work: Capitalizing on the Power of Diversity, (Alexandria, VA: Society for Human Resource Management, 2003) (*Internal Dimensions and External Dimensions are adapted from Marilyn Loden and Judy Rosener, Workforce America! Business One Irwin, 1991*)
5. Brenda Alvarez, *Why Social Justice in School Matters*, NEAToday, January 22, 2019, www.nea.org (last visited October 24, 2022).
6. Adapted from: Paul C. Gorski, gorski@earthlink.net, for **EdChange** and the *Multicultural Pavilion*, http://www.edchange.org, http://www.edchange.org/multicultural (last visited August 27, 2022).
7. Sarah Diem and Bradley W. Carpenter, *Social Justice & Leadership Preparation: Developing A Transformative Curriculum*, Planning and Changing, vol. 43, no. 1/2, 2012, at 96 – 112, 96. The authors assert that education leadership preparation programs should prepare their charges (*i.e.*, future teachers in increasingly diverse educational settings) to confront five key social justice challenges around race: (1) color-blind ideology; (2) misconceptions of human difference (*i.e.*, stereotypes); (3) merit-based achievement (*i.e.*, the myth of meritocracy); (4) critical self-reflection; and (5) the interrogation of race-based silences in the classroom.
8. David Rock and Heidi Grant, *Why Diverse Teams Are Smarter*, Harvard Business Review, November 4, 2016, hbr.org/2016/11/why-diverse-teams-are-smarter (last visited July 10, 2023).
9. John Howard Griffin, Black Like Me *(Boston, MA:* Houghton Mifflin, 1961). A "white ally" in today's parlance, Griffin was committed to social and racial justice and desirous of a better understanding of the lived experience of Black Americans. Griffin, a middle-aged white man in

Mansfield, Texas, began his odyssey in 1959. With financial backing from *Sepia Magazine*, this "white ally" tested the nation's seemingly indelible color line. He chemically altered his looks, using medication to darken his pale skin to deep brown—to turn him, essentially, from white to Black. Griffin set out on a southern journey, visiting Alabama, Arkansas, Georgia, Louisiana, and Mississippi to see how life might be different by virtue of how he was viewed through a racial lens. He discovered what many already knew: To be perceived as Black in the American South was to be treated, fundamentally and at best, as a second-class citizen. Griffin surrendered his white privilege for the harsh world of Black privation. He became an up-close witness to and a victim of the unrelenting, systemic racism that was a day-to-day reality for his born-Black brothers and sisters.

10. Amanda L. Tyler, *Lessons Learned From Justice Ruth Bader Ginsburg*, Columbia Law Review, vol. 121: RBG, https://www.columbialawreview.org/content/lessons-learned-from-justice-ruth-bader-ginsburg/ (last visited August 21, 2023).

## 5. 10 Ways We Can Advance Social Justice

1. *Elevate Society*, https://elevatesociety.com/freedom-is-incomplete-without-social/ (last visited August 21, 2023).
2. *Adapted from* Efrosini Costa, *10 ways to promote social justice everyday* (February 20, 2017), https://www.mindfood.com/article/promote-social-justice/ (last visited January 21, 2022).
3. Oxford Dictionaries (online) (last visited June 14, 2022).
4. *See, e.g.*, Patrice Brodeur, Rights, Responsibilities, and Skills of Dialogue, The Interfaith Observer, September 14, 2011, www.theinterfaithobserver.org/journal-articles/2011/9/14/rights-responsibilities-and-skills-of-dialogue.html (last visited April 24, 2022).
5. https://www.goodreads.com/quotes/98615-the-way-to-right-wrongs-is-to-turn-the-light (last visited August 21, 2023).
6. Engaging those with whom we disagree can be difficult. The phrase *"cancel culture"* refers, at least in part, to the large-scale withdrawal of engagement with and support for public figures or celebrities who have said or done things deemed socially unacceptable by the "canceling" individuals or groups. This "canceling" or mass shaming often occurs on social media platforms such as Twitter, Instagram, or Facebook, sometimes resulting in something akin to shunning or ostracism. Cancellation carries with it some risk of ignoring relevant perspectives and thwarting productive dialogue. Conversely, it arguably empowers people to boycott those who are perceived to be doing harm. Free speech arguments may be made on both sides of the cancel culture equation—for both the canceled and the canceling parties. *See, e.g.*, https://www.merriam-

webster.com/dictionary/cancel%20culture (last visited October 28, 2022).

7. *See, e.g., Listening to understand: How to practice active listening (with examples),* July 7, 2021, https://asana.com/resources/active-listening (last visited May 9, 2022).

8. E-mail from Kendall Trotter, Leadership Tulsa, June 9, 2022 (on file with author).

9. *Leadership Tulsa Favors Bond Issue,* Tulsa World, September 20, 1996 (updated February 25, 2019), https://tulsaworld.com/archive/leader ship-tulsa-favors-bond-issue/article_73b0cace-3ee9-507a-98f7-3b0d624a326d.html (last visited June 8, 2022).

10. Carmen J. Lee, Eleanor Chute, and Jane Elizabeth, *Tulsa superintendent gets top Pittsburgh job,* Post-Gazette.com, February 24, 2000, https://old.postgazette.com/neigh_city/20000224supt1.asp (last visited June 7, 2022).

11. Telephone conference with Wendy Thomas, Executive Director, Leadership Tulsa, June 7, 2022.

12. https://www.goodreads.com/work/quotes/65349561-the-woman-in-the-white-kimono (last visited August 21, 2023).

13. https://www.brainyquote.com/quotes/aaron_sorkin_426239 (last visited August 21, 2023).

14. *See, e.g.,* Omar Mateen, Counter Extremism Project, https://www.coun terextremism.com/extremists/omar-mateen (last visited June 17, 2022).

15. E-mail from Toby Jenkins to the author, June 15, 2022 (on file with author).

16. Community Dialogue Guide: Conducting a Discussion on Race, https://www.justice.gov/archive/crs/pubs/dialogueguide.pdf (last visited May 9, 2022).

17. Bill Moyers, *The Four Roles of Social Activism By Bill Moyers,* https://commonslibrary.org/the-four-roles-of-social-activism/ (last visited June 14, 2022).

18. https://www.thoughtco.com/coretta-scott-king-quotes-3530056 (last visited August 21, 2023).

19. *Adapted from* Charlene Costanzo, The Twelve Gifts of Birth (New York, NY HarperCollins, 2001). There are twelve birthright gifts: (1) **Strength**: Call upon it whenever you need it; (2) **Beauty**: Let your deeds reflect its depth; (3) **Courage**: Speak and act with confidence; use courage to follow your own path; (4) **Compassion**: Be gentle with yourself and others; forgive those who hurt you; forgive yourself when you make a mistake; (5) **Hope**: Trust the goodness of life through each passage and season; (6) **Joy**: Keep your heart open and filled with light; (7) **Talent**: Discover your own special abilities and contribute them toward a better world; (8) **Imagination**: Let it nourish your visions and dreams; (9) **Reverence**: Appreciate the wonder that you are and the miracle of all creation; (10) **Wisdom**: Hear the soft voice of wisdom that will guide your way through the knowledge and understanding; (11)

**Love**: Watch love grow each time you give it away; and (12) **Faith**: Believe.

20. The City of Tulsa is now a New Voices partner: "The New Voices Board Internship Program is offered in partnership with the Tulsa Area United Way and the City of Tulsa. All participants will have the opportunity to serve a one-year appointment on a TAUW agency board. Additionally, they will receive inside looks at the City of Tulsa's public Authorities, Boards and Commissions. Those successfully completing the program will have additional help with permanent board placements." Leadership Tulsa, https://leadershiptulsa.org/programs/new-voices/ (last visited September 5, 2022).

21. https://www.goodreads.com/quotes/11416-the-best-way-to-find-yourself-is-to-lose-yourself (last visited August 21, 2023).

22. Dr. Martin Luther King, Jr., *Letter from Birmingham Jail*, April 16, 1963, abacus.bates.edu/admin/offices/dos/mlk/letter.html (last visited May 8, 2022).

23. *See, e.g., 20 Social Justice Organizations to Support Right Now*, https://www.townandcountrymag.com/society/money-and-power/g32730417/george-floyd-blm-how-to-donate-help/ (last visited April 23, 2022); *see also, 10 Social Justice Organizations Fighting for Equality | Human Rights Careers* (last visited April 23, 2022).

24. The Say No To Hate Coalition has included the following organizations: the City of Tulsa Human Rights Department and Human Rights Commission, City of Tulsa Police Department, Community Service Council of Greater Tulsa, Coalition of Hispanic Organizations, Islamic Society of Tulsa, Jewish Federation of Tulsa, Oklahoma Center for Community and Justice, Oklahomans for Equality, PFLAG Tulsa, Tulsa City-County Library, Tulsa County Sheriff's Department, Tulsa Interfaith Alliance, Tulsa Metropolitan Ministry, Tulsa Public Schools, Union Public Schools, and YWCA Tulsa.

25. Bill Sherman, *Tulsa Coalition still saying no to hate, 25 years after founding*, Tulsa World, November 13, 2014 (updated February 19, 2019), https://tulsaworld.com/lifestyles/tulsa-coalition-still-saying-no-to-hate-25-years-after-founding/article_d3826b0e-485a-5355-9bc6-bdecfe3b-b633.html (last visited June 20, 2022).

26. *Goodreads.com*, https://www.goodreads.com/quotes/1062059-there-is-only-one-thing-worse-than-fighting-with-allies (last visited August 21, 2023).

27. James Baldwin, remarks delivered October 16, 1963, as *The Negro Child— His Self-Image*; originally published in The Saturday Review, December 21, 1963; excerpted from The Price of the Ticket (Boston, MA: Beacon Press, 2021).

28. A.J. Willingham, *21 ways to be politically active (whether you lean left or right)*, CNN Politics, January 23, 2017, https://www.cnn.com/2016/11/15/politics/ways-to-be-more-politically-active-trnd/index.html (last visited June 18, 2022).

29. R.L. Adams, *21 Famous Failures Who Refused to Give Up*, Huffpost, September 17, 2016, https://www.huffpost.com/entry/21-famous-failures-who-refused-to-give-up_b_57da2245e4b04fa361d991ba (last visited June 17, 2022).

30. https://www.brainyquote.com/topics/bragging-quotes (last visited August 21, 2023).

31. https://www.brainyquote.com/quotes/audre_lorde_390625 (last visited August 21, 2023).

32. *Adapted in part from*: San Diego State University, http://newscenter.sdsu.edu/lead/pledge_diversity.aspx (last visited August 17, 2016).

33. *Azquotes.com*, https://www.azquotes.com/quote/1544922 (last visited August 21, 2023).

34. *Adapted from* Efrosini Costa, *10 ways to promote social justice everyday*, February 20, 2017, https://www.mindfood.com/article/promote-social-justice/ (last visited January 21, 2022).

35. Edgar A. Guest, *Sermons We See;* Edgar Guest (1881-1959) worked for more than sixty years at the *Detroit Free Press* as a reporter and columnist. He published his first poem at the age of seventeen. Hundreds of American newspapers featured his work. He reportedly wrote some 11,000 poems during his lifetime. Critics often derided his work. Americans adored him, so much so that he was called the "People's Poet," served as Michigan's poet laureate, hosted a long-running radio show and television show, and published more than twenty books. *See, e.g.,* https://www.yourdailypoem.com/listpoem.jsp?poem_id=2270 (last visited April 26, 2022).

36. https://tulsachamber.com/missionvisionvalues (last visited June 16, 2022).

37. *Id.*

38. https://www.goodreads.com/quotes/26963-if-you-can-t-fly-then-run-if-you-can-t-run (last visited August 21, 2023).

39. *Understanding how children experience injustice*, World Vision, February 19, 2014, https://www.wvi.org/child-rights-and-equity/article/understanding-how-children-experience-injustice (last visited July 17, 2023).

40. Jinnie Spiegler, *Teaching Young Children About Bias, Diversity, and Social Justice*, Edutopia, June 16, 2016, https://www.edutopia.org/blog/teaching-young-children-social-justice-jinnie-spiegler (last visited July 16, 2023). Spiegler suggests using children's literature and the news media to teach kids about social justice. She also encourages the explicit teaching of anti-bias lessons, the use of concrete, familiar examples, and the exploration of solutions.

41. E-mail correspondence from Joseph Bojang to author, December 26, 2022.

42. https://www.brainyquote.com/quotes/abraham_lincoln_163082 (last visited August 21, 2023).

43. https://www.goodreads.com/quotes/tag/social-justice (last visited August 21, 2023).

## 6. Social Justice and the 1921 Tulsa Race Massacre: A Case Study

1. *Foreign Policy Association*, https://foreignpolicyblogs.com/2007/12/14/%E2%80%9Cit-is-from-numberless-diverse-acts-of-courage-and-belief-that-human-history-is-shaped-each-time-a-man-stands-up-for-an-ideal-or-acts-to-improve-the-lot-of-others-or-strikes-out-against-injust/ (last visited August 21, 2023) (excerpted from Robert F. Kennedy's "Day of Affirmation" address at the University of Capetown, South Africa, on June 6, 1966).

2. *See, e.g.*, Resmaa Menakem, My Grandmother's Hands: Racialized Traum and the Pathway to Mending Our Hearts and Bodies (Las Vegas, NV: Central Recovery Press, 2017). In My Grandmother's Hands, the phrase "white-body supremacy" focuses attention on the near-reflexive, often unconscious, preference given whiteness over blackness and the devasting, generation-spanning effects of that bias. Resmaa Menakem writes: "Ideally, America will grow up and out of white-body supremacy; Americans will begin healing their long-held trauma around race; and whiteness will begin to evolve from race to culture, and then to community." *Id.* at xviii.

3. Tulsa's numbers swelled between 1900 and 1920 as it emerged as the "Oil Capital." The 1910 census lists 18,182 inhabitants and the 1920 census pegs Tulsa's population at 109,023. Of these numbers, the Black population comprised some 5 – 10%. *See, e.g., Oklahoma Census: 1910 & 1920: Volume 1: Detailed Tables*, The University of Tulsa, McFarlin Library, https://libraries.utulsa.edu/okcensus/okcensus1920 (last visited August 22, 2023).

4. *Park is fitting memorial to 1921*, Tulsa World (editorial), November 19, 2008 (updated February 11, 2019), https://tulsaworld.com/news/local/race-massacre/painful-past/article_b2ab58ea-bf19-5cfd-b3c3-492a28b752a1.html (last visited June 15, 2022).

5. "Red Summer" refers to a period in 1919 during which a series of race-based incidents of civil unrest, routinely labeled "race riots," occurred. Between May and October of that year, violent assaults on African American communities took place in more than two dozen American cities, including: Chicago; Washington D.C.; Longview, Texas; Omaha, Nebraska; and Elaine, Arkansas. Several factors precipitated the racial tumult, including the systemic, institutional racism so prevalent in the era. Other triggers included three principal, related dynamics: (1) Labor shortages in Northern and Midwestern factories occasioned by white male enlistment in World War I at a time when European immigration had been curtailed; (2) The Great Migration of African Americans from the Deep South to Northern and Midwestern cities to fill job vacancies and, simultaneously, escape the social, economic, and political oppression characteristic of the Deep South; and (3) racial resentment, based on

economic competition, on the part of working class white Americans in the Northern and Midwestern cities to which African Americans migrated. Femi Lewis, *The Red Summer of 1919: Race Riots Rock Cities Throughout the United States,* https://www.thoughtco.com/red-summer-of-1919-45394 (last visited May 2, 2019).

6. *Reconnecting neighborhoods: Don't forget Greenwood when seeking infrastructure funds* (editorial), Tulsa World, August 27, 2022, at A7.

7. Senator Matthews grew up just blocks from the Greenwood District and still lives nearby. Telephone conversation between Senator Kevin Matthews and the author, August 22, 2023.

8. Susan Ellingwood, *What Is Critical Race Theory, and Why Is Everyone Talking About It?: Columbia Law School professors explain this method of research for legal scholars and how it's being misunderstood,* Columbia News, July 1, 2021, https://news.columbia.edu/news/what-critical-race-theory-and-why-everyone-talking-about-it-0 (last visited July 8, 2022).

9. Bill Text: OK HB1775 | 2021 | Regular Session | Enrolled, May 10, 2021; Approved by Governor, May 7, 2021, https://legiscan.com/OK/text/HB1775/id/2387002 (last visited July 7, 2022); *Stitt signs HB 1775 prohibiting certain types of teaching about race,* May 8, 2021, https://freepres sokc.com/stitt-signs-hb1775-prohibiting-certain-types-of-teaching-about-race/ (last visited July 7, 2022).

10. *Board decision arbitrary, unfair: Vote on TPS illustrates pitfalls of poorly written HB 1775* (editorial), Tulsa World, August 13, 2022.

11. *OUR VIEW: Time to toss out House Bill 1775* (editorial), Stillwater News Press, August 11, 2022, https://www.stwnewspress.com/opinion/our-view-time-to-toss-out-house-bill-1775/article_b3cf890a-18f0-11ed-976f-6f9fcc15bae6.html?eType=EmailBlastContent&eId=f82872e7-cd2e-407c-9021-702ff10d97ba (last visited August 15, 2022).

12. Senator Kevin Matthews, Letter to the Editor, December 31, 2018 (on file with author).

13. *The Case for Reparations,* the 1921 Tulsa Race Massacre Centennial Commission (press statement, March 26, 2021).

14. 1921 Tulsa Race Massacre Centennial Commission, press release for the Greenwood Art Project, January 15, 2019 (on file with author).

15. 1921 Tulsa Race Massacre Centennial Commission press release, June 12, 2020 (on file with author).

16. Glenn E. Singleton and Curtis Linton, Courageous Conversations About Race: A Field Guide for Achieving Equity in Schools (Thousand Oaks, CA: Sage Publications, Inc., 2005).

17. The Law Dictionary (featuring Black's Law Dictionary Free Online Legal Dictionary 2nd ed.) https://thelawdictionary.org/damages/ (last visited May 14, 2022.

18. *Oklahoma history standard, Content Standard 4.2 (1920s through 1940s):* "Examine multiple points of view regarding the historic evolution of race relations in Oklahoma including Senate Bill 1 establishing Jim Crow laws, the growth of all-Black towns, the Tulsa Race Riot and the resur-

gence of the Ku Klux Klan." *U.S. history standard, Content Standard 3.1b (1920s and 1930s):* "Describe the rising racial tensions in American society, including the resurgence of the Ku Klux Klan, increased lynchings, race riots as typified by the Tulsa Race Riot, and the use of poll taxes and literacy tests to disenfranchise blacks and poor whites." *See also,* Randy Krehbiel, *Once taboo discussion, Tulsa Race Riot now included in state academic standards,* Tulsa World, May 31, 2016, https://tulsaworld.com/news/local/education/once-taboo-discussion-tulsa-race-riot-now-included-in-state-academic-standards/article_9f6dfdd5-1fd7-58b4-9c06-b047c7ebe31e.html (last visited July 8, 2022).

19. Hannibal B. Johnson, *What I've Learned Teaching the Tulsa Race Massacre for Two Decades,* New York Times, May 31, 2021, www.nytimes.com/2021/05/31/opinion/tulsa-race-massacre-teaching-history.html (last visited June 11, 2022).

20. Nuria Martinez-Keel, *'A conspiracy of silence': Tulsa Race Massacre was absent from schools for generations,* The Oklahoman, May 26, 2021, https://www.oklahoman.com/story/news/education/2021/05/26/oklahoma-history-black-wall-street-left-out-public-schools-tulsa-massacre-education/4875340001/ (last visited July 8, 2022).

21. https://www.okhistory.org/research/forms/freport.pdf    Oklahoma Historical Society (last visited August 15, 2022).

22. *Lessie Benningfield Randle, et al. v. City of Tulsa, et al.,* No. CV-2020-01179 (Tulsa County D.C. 2020).

23. Randy Krehbiel, *Race Massacre survivors to appeal suit's dismissal,* Tulsa World, July 11, 2023, at A-1.

24. *Tulsa Releases 2021 Equality Indicators Scores, Covid-19 Community Impact Survey Findings, Data for Action Resource Guide,* December 8, 2021 (archived January 9, 2022), https://www.cityoftulsa.org/press-room/2021-equality-indicators-scores-available/ (last visited July 18, 2022). Tulsa's 2021 rating on the "justice" indicator was 30.78/100, down some 4.5 points from the 2018 baseline. Components of that composite justice score showed mixed results. Hispanic representation in the Tulsa Police Department increased from the 2018 baseline average. However, "safety" and "violence" dropped 7.67 points from the 2018 baseline, attributable largely to increases in the disparity between Tulsa and the nation in child abuse and neglect, and in homicide victimization by race. Both indicators showed improvement over the 2020 scores. The "juvenile arrests by race" indicator came in at 20, down by 13 points from both the 2018 baseline and from the 2020 report.

25. *Tulsa mayor calls for probe into possible mass graves from 1921 race riot,* CBSnews.com, October 3, 2018, https://www.cbsnews.com/news/tulsa-mayor-gt-bynum-investigation-possible-mass-graves-1921-race-riot/ (last visited July 12, 2022).

26. Kevin Canfield, *City Council approves resolution apologizing for Tulsa Race Massacre, committing to tangible amends,* Tulsa World, June 3, 2021 (updated July 10, 2021), https://tulsaworld.com/news/local/racemassacre/coun

cil-approves-resolution-apologizing-for-tulsa-race-massacre-committing-to-tangible-amends/article_36848552-c344-11eb-bee2-e7d746c8e4b3.html (last visited March 22, 2022); Kevin Canfield, *Mayor G.T. Bynum signs resolution creating community-led process to discuss possible Race Massacre redress,* https://tulsaworld.com/news/local/govt-and-politics/mayor-bynum-signs-resolution-creating-community-led-process-to-discuss-possible-race-massacre-redress/article_0ef80002-bc33-11ec-901f-ebdc383fddeb.html (last visited April 18, 2022).

27. *Editorial: 100 years after the Tulsa Race Massacre, the City Council apologizes,* Tulsa World
(June 6, 2021, updated July 13, 2021), https://tulsaworld.com/opinion/editorial/editorial-100-years-after-the-tulsa-race-massacre-the-city-council-apologizes/article_cda1aae8-c491-11eb-b647-3bdd14cf24a6.html (last visited March 22, 2022); *see also Editorial: Council resolution on race massacre a step forward toward real action,* Tulsa World, April 19, 2022 (updated April 20, 2022), https://tulsaworld.com/opinion/editorial/editorial-council-resolution-on-race-massacre-a-step-toward-real-action/article_3b2db41e-c02f-11ec-803e-c7e615dc4288.html (last visited April 20, 2022) .

28. *See, e.g., Advocating for Teaching Honest History: What Educators Can Do, Learning for Justice,* learningforjustice.org/Advocate-THH-Fall22 (last visited November 3, 2022).

29. http://www.azquotes.com/quote/391706 (last visited December 3, 2023).

## Conclusion

1. https://www.brainyquote.com/quotes/martin_luther_king_jr_164280 (last visited August 21, 2023).

2. https://www.brainyquote.com/quotes/helen_keller_132599 (last visited August 21, 2023).

## Appendix A

1. For additional information on social justice resources, *see, e.g.,* Jennifer Gonzalez, *A Collection of Resources for Teaching Social Justice,* Cult of Pedagogy, February 14, 2012, https://www.cultofpedagogy.com/social-justice-resources/ (last visited May 2, 2022).

2. *See Social Justice Organizations,* https://startguide.org/orgs/orgs06.html (last visited April 23, 2022).

## Appendix B

1. Robin N. Hamilton, *What Social Justice Looks Like—What We Need And Why*, Around Robin (February 1, 2022), https://www.aroundrobin.com/social-justice-issues/ (last visited April 25, 2022).
2. Letter from Harvard University President Lawrence S. Bacow to Harvard alumni referencing Harvard and the legacy of slavery, April 26, 2022 (on file with author).
3. *H.R. 40: Commission to Study and Develop Reparation Proposals for African Americans Act*, HR40 (117ᵗʰ), https://www.govtrack.us/congress/bills/117/hr40/cosponsors (last visited July 12, 2022).
4. Rob Bonta, Attorney General, State of California Department of Justice, Press Release: *California Reparations Task Force Releases Interim Report Detailing Harms of Slavery and Systemic Discrimination on African Americans*, June 1, 2022; interim report at https://oag.ca.gov/system/files/media/ab3121-reparations-interim-report-2022.pdf (last visited December 12, 2022).

## Appendix C

1. Adapted from Maurianne Adams, Lee Ann Bell, and Pat Griffin, Teaching for Diversity and Social Justice—A Sourcebook (New York and London: Routledge, 1997), p. 140.Introspection, awareness, compassion, and empathy are among the key elements needed to foster diversity and promote an inclusive community. Transformational change, however, requires a personal commitment to positive action. Transformational change requires leadership.

# ABOUT THE AUTHOR

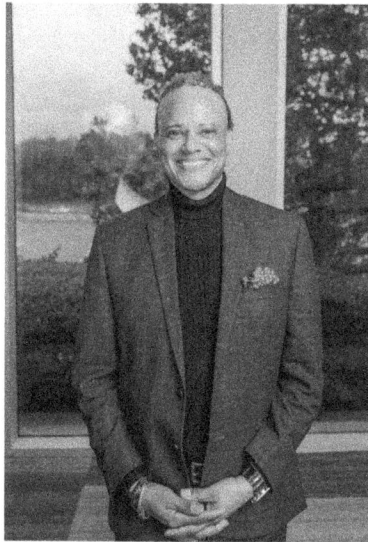

HANNIBAL B. JOHNSON, a Harvard Law School graduate, is an author, attorney, and consultant specializing in DEI, human relations, leadership, and non-profit governance. He hails from Fort Smith, Arkansas, and graduated from the University of Arkansas, Fayetteville, with a double major in Economics and Sociology.

Johnson has taught at The University of Tulsa College of Law, Oklahoma State University, and The University of Oklahoma. He serves on the federal 400 Years of African American History Commission and chairs its Economics and Diversity, Equity & Inclusion Committee. Johnson chaired the

Education Committee for the 1921 Tulsa Race Massacre Centennial Commission and served as local curator of its world-class history center, Greenwood Rising.

Johnson's books, including *Black Wall Street 100: An American City Grapples With Its Historical Racial Trauma*, chronicle the African American experience in Oklahoma and its indelible impact on American history. Johnson's play, *Big Mama Speaks— A Tulsa Race Riot Survivor's Story*, was selected for the 2011 National Black Theatre Festival and has been staged in Caux, Switzerland.

Johnson has received numerous honors and awards for his work and community service, including a lifetime achievement award from the Oklahoma Center for the Book and induction into the Oklahoma Historians Hall of Fame, the Tulsa Hall of Fame, and the Oklahoma Hall of Fame.

## ALSO BY HANNIBAL B. JOHNSON

*Black Wall Street 100: An American City Grapples with its Historical Racial Trauma*

*Black Wall Street: From Riot to Renaissance in Tulsa's Historic Greenwood District*

*Images of America: Tulsa's Historic Greenwood District*

*Acres of Aspiration: The All-Black Towns in Oklahoma*

*Up From the Ashes*

*Mama Used to Say: Wit & Wisdom from the Heart & Soul*

*Apartheid in Indian Country?: Seeing Red Over Black Disenfranchisement*

*IncogNegro: Poetic Reflections on Race & Diversity in America*

*No Place Like Home: A Story About An All-Black, All-American Town*

*The Sawners of Chandler: A Pioneering Power Couple in Pre-Civil Rights Oklahoma*

www.ingramcontent.com/pod-product-compliance
Lightning Source LLC
Chambersburg PA
CBHW031358180326
41458CB00043B/6538/J